OWN IT! 3

PROJECT BOOK

Simon Cupit

CAMBRIDGE
UNIVERSITY PRESS

CAMBRIDGE
UNIVERSITY PRESS & ASSESSMENT

Shaftesbury Road, Cambridge CB2 8EA, United Kingdom

One Liberty Plaza, 20th Floor, New York, NY 10006, USA

477 Williamstown Road, Port Melbourne, VIC 3207, Australia

314–321, 3rd Floor, Plot 3, Splendor Forum, Jasola District Centre, New Delhi – 110025, India

103 Penang Road, #05–06/07, Visioncrest Commercial, Singapore 238467

José Abascal, 56–1°, 28003 Madrid, Spain

Cambridge University Press & Assessment is a department of the University of Cambridge.

We share the University's mission to contribute to society through the pursuit of education, learning and research at the highest international levels of excellence.

www.cambridge.org
Information on this title: www.cambridge.org/9781108726634

First published 2020

20 19 18 17 16 15 14 13 12 11 10 9 8 7 6

Printed in Great Britain by Ashford Colour Press Ltd.

A catalogue record for this publication is available from the British Library

ISBN 978-1-108-72663-4 Own it! Project Book Level 3
ISBN 978-8-413-22012-3 Collaborate Project Book Level 3

Additional resources for this publication at www.cambridge.org/ownit/resources

CONTENTS

An introduction to project work 4

Benefits and advantages of project work 5

Project work and the Cambridge Life Competencies Framework 6

How to use the Project book 8

The learning stages of project work 10

L1 in project work 11

Mixed abilities in project work 12

Time management in project work 14

Challenges and implications 15

Collaboration 16

Presentation ideas 18

Evaluation 20

Evaluation rubric 21

1 The culture project

A presentation 22

2 The art project

A profile of an artist 26

3 The culture project

A language fact file 30

4 The PE project

A report 34

5 The culture project

A magazine article 38

6 The technology project

A presentation 42

7 The culture project

A travel blog 46

8 The citizenship project

A timeline 50

9 The culture project

A poster 54

Print materials 58

Presentation organiser 58

Profile organiser 59

Language fact file organiser 60

Report organiser 61

Magazine article organiser 62

Invention organiser 63

Travel blog organiser 64

Brochure organiser 65

Poster organiser 66

KWL chart 67

My learning diary 68

Peer-evaluation form 69

Teacher's evaluation form 70

My time-management plan 71

Acknowledgements 72

AN INTRODUCTION TO PROJECT WORK

Welcome back! Are you ready for another year of rewarding challenges in your English class? How are you going to help your students develop their skills this year?

Your students should now be used to project work and be familiar with its different stages: preparation, development and production. They are now ready to expand their language skills and will be able to use more English as they plan, discuss and think about their work. The projects in Level 3 are designed to help your students improve and stay motivated.

This book will guide you on how to make the most of different projects, so your students can continue to work successfully both in and out of the classroom.

What is project work?

Imagine you and your class have just finished Unit 6 (*Think outside the box*). Your students have learned vocabulary for making things and materials and practised giving and following instructions. How can you review and build on this topic? In this case, your students give a presentation of an idea for an invention, including a description of what it is made from, how it works and what problem it solves.

Remember that project work involves students being responsible for their work and making decisions together. There is a realistic final outcome and a series of stages to follow that allow groups to explore how they can achieve their goals. The final aim is always a presentation stage. > Presentation ideas p18. Your role is to help this happen. As a result, students learn by doing and share experiences.

Throughout the project work process, students develop a number of **life skills**. They learn to:

BENEFITS AND ADVANTAGES OF PROJECT WORK

Personal advantages

- encourages **creativity** by promoting **different ways of thinking**
- increases **motivation** through challenge
- develops **independence** and a **sense of responsibility**
- increases natural **curiosity**
- improves **self-knowledge** through **self-evaluation**
- improves **communication skills** through teamwork
- involves family and friends in the **learning process**
- improves **interpersonal** relationships
- develops **life skills**

Academic advantages

- allows teachers to deal with **mixed-ability** classes
- motivates whole-team / cooperation / group work and promotes chances to **learn from one another**
- develops **planning** and **organisational skills**
- permits a '**flipped classroom**' approach
- **helps learning** through research and opportunities for deep thinking
- increases opportunities to **integrate cross-curricular** and **cultural topics**
- encourages **peer teaching** and **correction**
- enables students with **different learning styles** to help one another

Language learning

- provides opportunities to **use language naturally**
- integrates all **four skills** (reading, writing, listening and speaking)
- allows for the use of **self- and peer-evaluation language**
- encourages research and **use of English out of the class**
- is learner-centred: students **learn language from one another**
- practises both **fluency** and **accuracy** through different types of presentations

Project work and the Cambridge Life Competencies Framework

How can we prepare our students to succeed in a changing world? We see the need to help students develop transferable skills, to work with people from around the globe, to think creatively, analyse sources critically and communicate their views. However, how can we balance the development of these skills with the demands of the language curriculum?

Cambridge have developed the Cambridge Life Competencies Framework. This Framework reinforces project work, helping teachers recognise and assess the many transferable skills that project work develops, alongside language learning.

The Framework provides different levels of detail, from six broad Competencies to specific Can Do Statements. The Competencies are supported by three foundation layers.

Critical Thinking	Creative Thinking	Collaboration	Communication	Learning to Learn	Social Responsibilities
EMOTIONAL DEVELOPMENT AND WELLBEING		DIGITAL LITERACY		DISCIPLINE KNOWLEDGE	

It then defines specific Core Areas. For example, here are the Core Areas for Collaboration.

Taking personal responsibility for own contribution to a group task.	Listening respectfully and responding constructively to others' contributions.	Managing the sharing of tasks in a project.	Working towards a resolution related to a task.

Then, there is a Can Do Statement for each Core Area. These will differ depending on the age of the students.

Competency
Collaboration

Core Area
Managing the sharing of tasks in a project.

Can Do Statements
- Follows the instructions for a task and alerts others when not following them.
- Explains reasons for suggestions and contributions.
- Takes responsibility for completing tasks as part of a larger project.

For more information, go to: cambridge.org/elt

Level 3 Projects	Competency	Core Area	Can Do Statements
1 The culture project: a presentation Teacher's Resource Bank Unit 1	Critical Thinking	Evaluating ideas, arguments and options	*Analyses causes and effects of problems; Examines possible solutions to a given problem and states how effective they are.*
	Communication	Managing conversations	*Uses appropriate strategies to deal with language gaps (using non-linguistic means, approximate synonyms, etc.); Invites contributions from interlocuters in a conversation.*
2 The art project: a profile of an artist Student's Book pp30–31	Learning to Learn	Taking control of your own learning	*Finds sources of information and help (online); Chooses ways to practise English outside the classroom (e.g. watching TV/ films in English, using English on social media).*
	Creative Thinking	Creating new content from own ideas or other resources	*Makes an assignment original by changing the task or adding new angles; Communicates personal response to creative work from art, music or literature.*
3 The culture project: a fact file Teacher's Resource Bank Unit 3	Learning to Learn	Practical skills for participating in learning	*Completes homework as required; Takes effective notes in class and from homework reading.*
	Collaboration	Managing the sharing of tasks in a project	*Participates with others to plan, organise and carry out events; Ensures that work is fairly divided among members in group activities.*
4 The PE project: a report Student's Book pp54–55	Critical Thinking	Evaluating ideas, arguments and options	*Gives reasons for an argument's plausibility; Assesses strengths and weaknesses of possible solutions.*
	Communication	Managing conversations	*Uses appropriate language to negotiate meaning (seek repetition, check understanding); Uses simple techniques to start, maintain and close conversations of various lengths.*
5 The culture project: a magazine article Teacher's Resource Bank Unit 5	Social Responsibilities	Understanding personal responsibilities as part of a group and in society	*Understands the rights and responsibilities of individuals in society at local and national levels; Understands various aspects of society.*
	Creative Thinking	Participating in creative activities	*Encourages group members to make activities more original and imaginative; Participates in 'what if' thinking.*
6 The technology project: a presentation Student's Book pp78–79	Collaboration	Working towards a resolution related to a task	*Is aware others have divergent views and ideas for solving a task; Is able to propose solutions that include other views and ideas than their own.*
	Communication	Participating with appropriate confidence and clarity	*Develops a clear description or narrative with a logical sequence of points; Uses a number of cohesive devices to link sentences into a clear, coherent discourse.*
7 The culture project: a travel blog Teacher's Resource Bank Unit 7	Social Responsibilities	Understanding and describing own and others' cultures	*Accepts others and shows respect for cultural difference, challenges prejudice and discriminatory views; Makes informed comparisons between their own and other societies.*
	Creative Thinking	Using newly created content to solve problems and make decisions	*Employs new ideas and content in solving a task; Makes an assignment original by changing the task or adding new angles.*
8 The citizenship project: a school brochure Student's Book pp102–103	Collaboration	Listening respectfully and responding constructively to others' contributions	*Listens to and acknowledges different points of view respectfully; Is ready to justify, adapt and abandon a proposal or point of view in response to others' queries or contributions.*
	Critical Thinking	Synthesising ideas and information	*Selects key points from diverse sources to create a new account and/or argument.*
9 The culture project: a poster Teacher's Resource Bank Unit 9	Social Responsibilities	Understanding and discussing global issues	*Is aware of different global issues; Understands the importance of international cooperation.*
	Learning to Learn	Practical skills for participating in learning	*Completes homework as required; Participates sensibly and positively in learning activities in class.*

HOW TO USE THE PROJECT BOOK

See learning outcomes, as well as the skills students will develop and the resources and evaluation tools you may wish to use.

Manage student roles and responsibilities.

Get useful tips for monitoring collaborative skills.

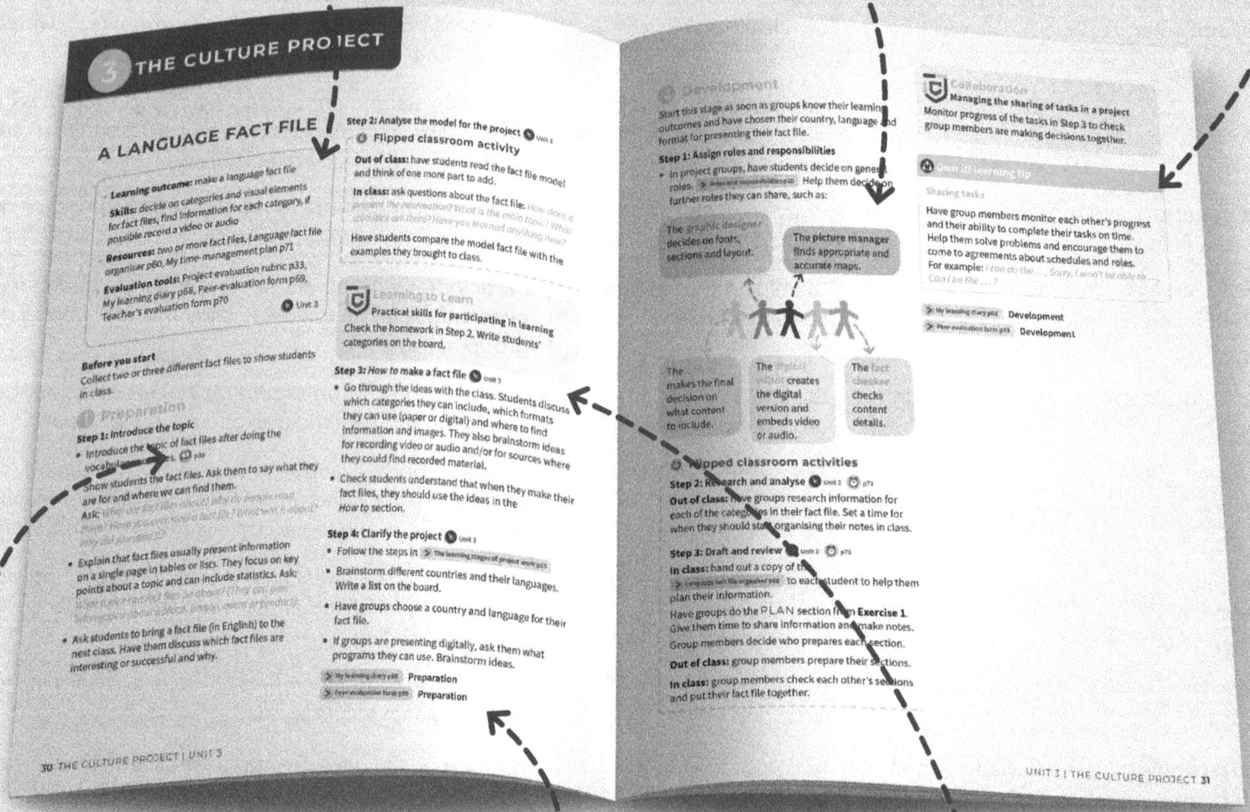

Identify the correct part of the Student's Book.

Find useful photocopiable resources.

Monitor and check the skills that project work develops, mapped to the Cambridge Life Competencies Framework.

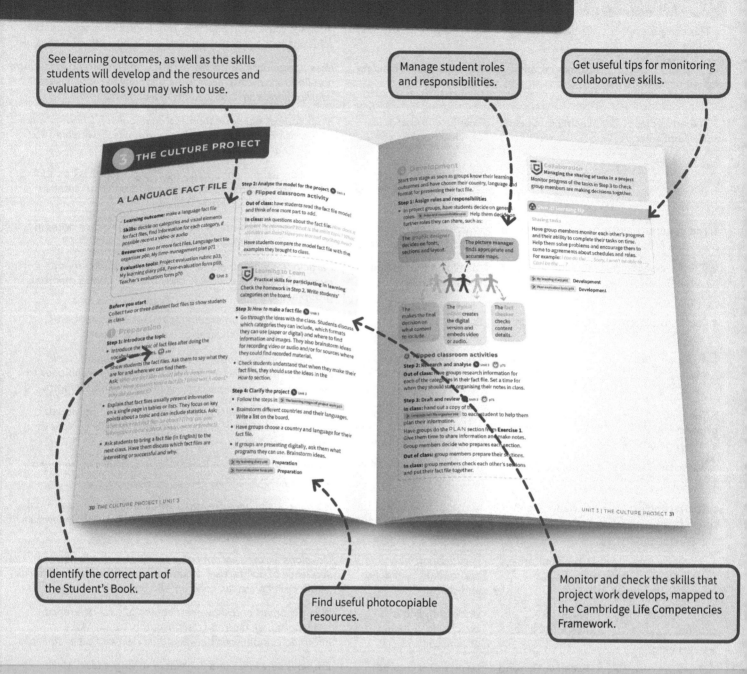

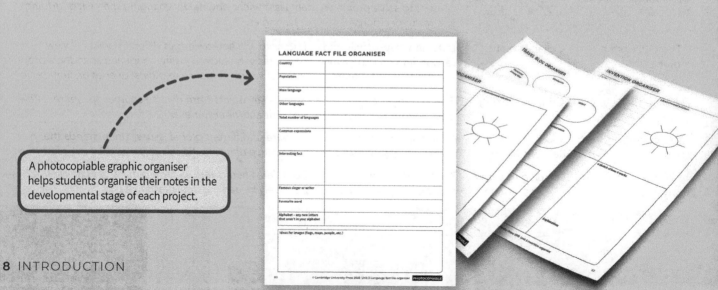

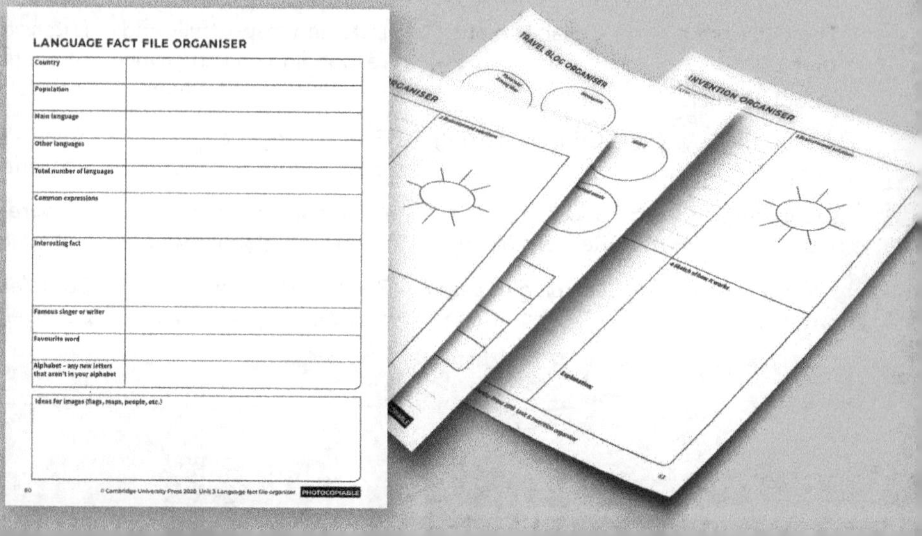

A photocopiable graphic organiser helps students organise their notes in the developmental stage of each project.

Get ideas for extra practice in each project; perfect for mixed abilities!

See clear guidelines for identifying and checking student performance.

Identify the other important skills that project work develops.

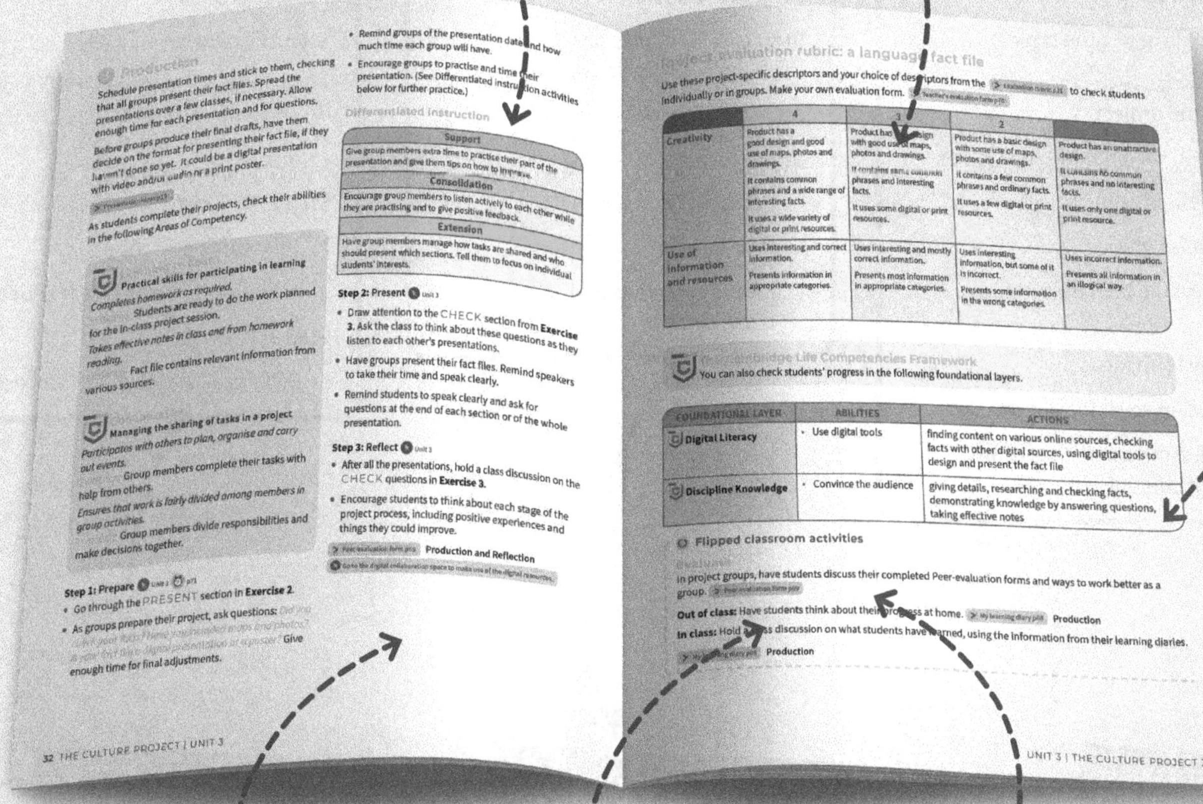

Students can work together on their projects in the digital collaboration space, and teachers can track and assess their work. Students can also share and comment on each other's work in the portfolio.

Help students check themselves and their peers.

Get flipped-classroom ideas for carrying out the activities both in and out of class.

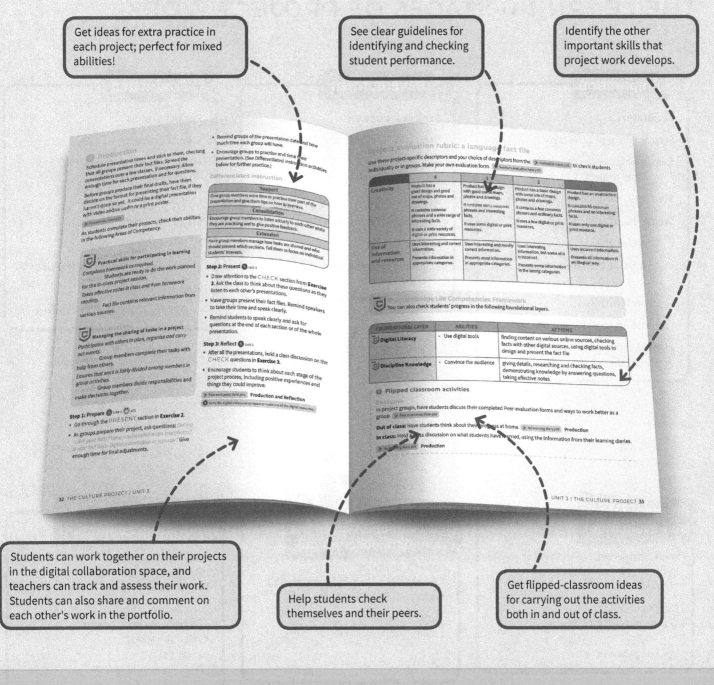

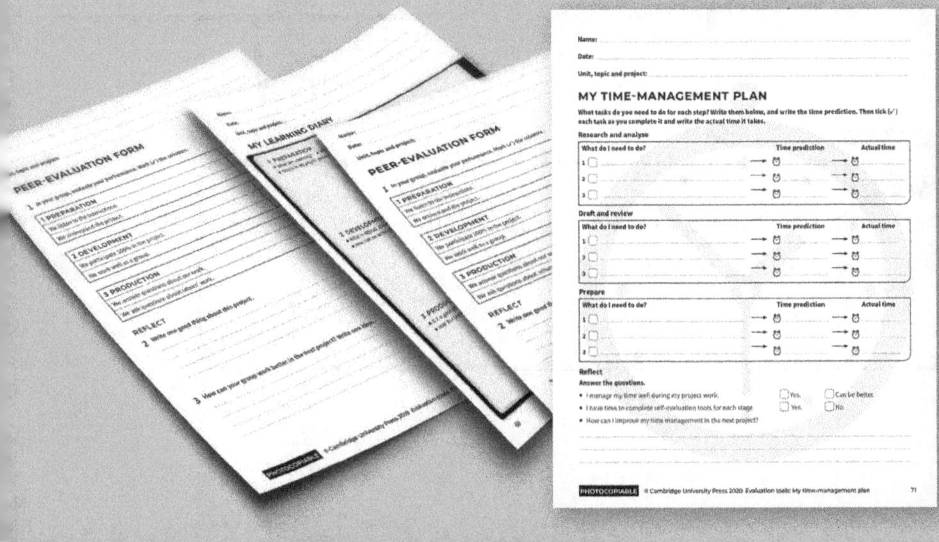

Photocopiable assessment and time-management sheets help students work more independently.

THE LEARNING STAGES OF PROJECT WORK

1 Preparation

Facilitators

Step 1: Introduce the topic

Step 2: Analyse the model for the project

Step 3: Go through the *How to* tips

Step 4: Clarify the project

- Organise groups
- Review the learning outcomes and skills
- Brainstorm ideas
- Focus on key information
- Have groups make decisions about content

2 Development

Project groups

Step 1: Assign roles and responsibilities

Step 2: Research and analyse

Step 3: Draft and review

- Put together work
- Peer-correct
- Express opinions and make choices

3 Production

Project groups

Step 1: Prepare

- Decide how the project will look and who will speak
- Practise

Step 2: Present

- Take turns presenting
- Ask questions and give feedback

Step 3: Reflect

- Discuss all stages of the process

Pre-evaluation (self-evaluation)

Tools for students:
KWL chart, My learning diary, Peer-evaluation form

Tools for teachers:
Teacher's evaluation form

> Evaluation tools pp67–70

Formative evaluation (self-evaluation, peer-evaluation, observation)

Tools for students:
KWL chart, My learning diary, graphic organisers, Peer-evaluation form

Tools for teachers:
Teacher's evaluation form

> Evaluation tools pp67–70

Formative and summative evaluation

Tools for students:
KWL chart, My learning diary, Peer-evaluation form

Tools for teachers:
Teacher's evaluation form, Evaluation rubric

> Evaluation tools pp67–70

> Evaluation rubric p21

Reflection (you and students)

1 Have *student-to-student*, *student-to-teacher* and *teacher-to-student* discussions on evaluation grades.

2 Identify areas for improvement in future projects using the Evaluation tools.

> Evaluation p20

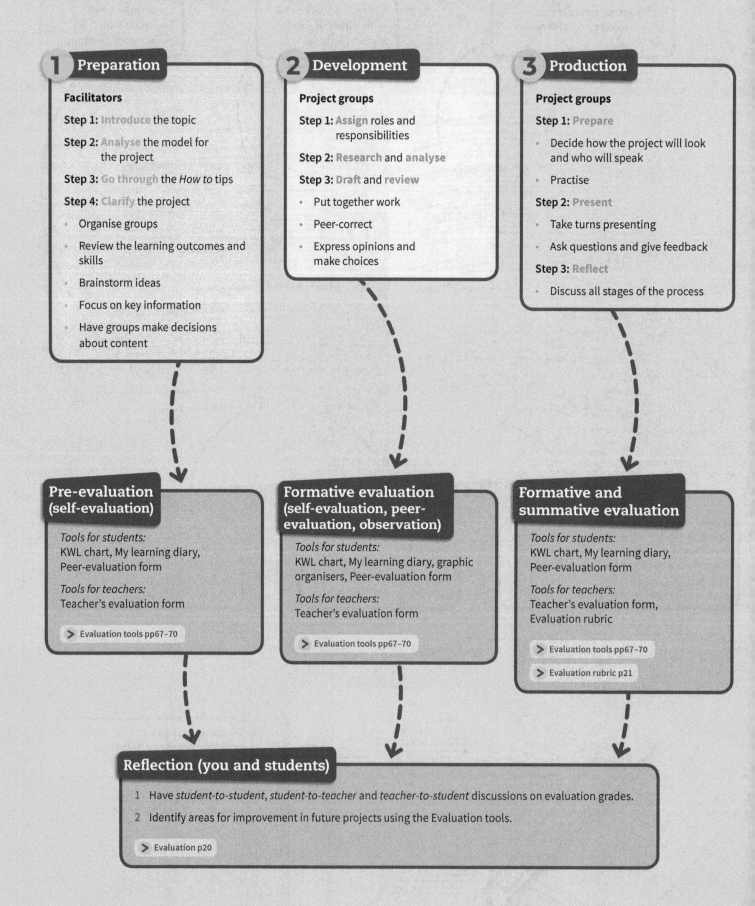

L1 IN PROJECT WORK

Many teachers believe that the only way for students to learn English effectively is by using it at all times in class. They feel that any time students spend using their own language is a missed opportunity.

Do you allow L1 use in your classroom? If you do, don't worry: there is little data to support the above idea (Kerr, 2016)[1]. In fact, there are occasions when allowing students to use L1 is positive. This is particularly true of project work.

We can use L1 in different steps of the project cycle. Take *Clarify the project* as an example (Preparation stage, Step 4). If students fail to understand the project's objectives, they won't carry it out properly. Allowing L1 use is not a 'missed opportunity' here. It ensures a richer project experience.

Of course, this doesn't mean you should use students' own language *all* of the time. You have to consider factors like age, level, the difficulty of the project and its outcomes. The question is not *if* you should use own language, but *when*, *how* and *how much*.

At Level 3, we suggest you allow own-language use for in-depth explanations. However, encourage more use of English during discussions, in addition to the development and presentation stages.

- Set rules for when students can use L1.
- Encourage groups to monitor their own-language use and explore English equivalents.
- Allow students 'own-language moments' (Kerr, 2014: 26–29)[2], such as preparing for speaking activities. Remember that the students' goal is to produce English in the Production stage of project work.

OL = Own language, E = English, shows suggested language

THE LEARNING STAGES OF PROJECT WORK		
1 Preparation	OL	E
Introducing and discussing the topic		
Analysing the model for the project		
Going through the *How to* tips		
Clarifying the project		
2 Development	OL	E
Assigning roles and responsibilities		
Researching and analysing		
Drafting and reviewing		
3 Production	OL	E
Preparing the final presentation		
Presenting the project		
Reflecting on the process		

[1] Kerr, Philip (2016). 'The learner's own language'. *Explorations in English Language and Linguistics*. 3.1: 1–7
[2] Kerr, Philip (2014). *Translation and Own-language Activities*. Cambridge: Cambridge University Press.

MIXED ABILITIES IN PROJECT WORK

How can you teach in ways that suit each type of learner? Projects offer a great advantage in this area, as students can explore different ways of completing them.

Mixed-ability classes can depend on individual differences such as motivation, ability, age and experience. Allow your students to express their ideas in different ways, and remember that no one will be happy with a project that is too difficult or too easy.

Studies have shown that adolescence is the best time for instructed language learning. Teenagers are faster at learning and are ready to understand and use rules (DeKeyser, 2010)[1]. Your activities should reflect this, which means getting to know your students and their differences in the following four areas:

Cognitive maturity

Your students' ages and experiences affect their ability to understand and follow instructions.

→ Adapt instructions according to level and avoid complicated words and phrases with beginners and elementary students.

Proficiency

Every member of your class will have a different language level.

→ Make sure tasks involve an appropriate degree of difficulty and are suitably challenging. Provide the levels of support needed.

Interests

Teenagers have a wide variety of interests and skills.

→ Allow students to take roles within a project that help them develop their personal interests and relate to the main task. Encourage them to expand their knowledge.

Learning preferences

Everyone has different learning preferences, such as reading, taking notes, asking questions, listening, moving around or watching videos.

→ Use a variety of learning styles in your classroom, such as visual, aural, verbal, physical or logical.

The roles of the facilitator

Give feedback

Is it a mouse?

Ask for and give reasons

Why? Because ...

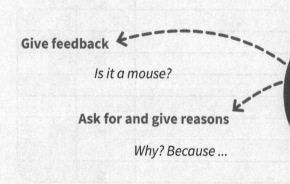

Encourage participation

What do you think?

Listen actively

That's interesting! Really?

[1] DeKeyser, R., Alfi-Shabtay, I., & Ravid, D. (2010). 'Cross-linguistic evidence for the nature of age effects in second language acquisition'. *Applied Psycholinguistics*, 31(3), 413–438.

Classroom suggestions

Challenge	Suggestion
When working in groups, stronger students solve the problems, while others stay quiet.	Allow time for 'think, pair, share' activities, where students think individually first, discuss ideas with a partner, then share with another pair.
When weaker students are put in groups according to ability, they become labelled as 'less proficient', which affects their motivation and self-esteem.	Change groups to make sure all students benefit and contribute in different contexts.
High-ability students do not feel challenged.	Give extension work and higher-level input.
Weaker students do not complete tasks.	Give additional support and adapted activities.

Differentiated instruction

We provide a specific suggestion for differentiated instruction in each project.
Each one has three categories:

1. *Support* activities help students to better understand the tasks and concepts
2. *Consolidation* activities reinforce what students are learning
3. *Extension* activities provide additional challenges for more proficient students.

1 PREPARATION		
Support	**Consolidation**	**Extension**
Suggest ways to record and keep notes. Extend time limits. Give specific goals related to competencies.	Have students organise ideas. Provide specific tasks to improve competencies. Give extra roles and responsibilities.	Suggest alternative ideas. Focus on additional competencies. Set additional goals.

2 DEVELOPMENT		
Support	**Consolidation**	**Extension**
Provide more examples of models. Suggest sources for research. Give essential information that helps with students' roles. Ask specific questions about findings.	Analyse different models. Have students share opinions. Make additional notes of findings. Check sources. Give extra responsibility in line with roles.	Produce another model for the project. Analyse opinions. Look for different points of view. Allow for peer-teaching.

3 PRODUCTION		
Support	**Consolidation**	**Extension**
Ensure level-appropriate participation during presentation. Allow feedback in own language. Suggest ways to improve.	Encourage feedback in English. Have students discuss self-evaluation. Encourage suggestions for ways to improve.	Give all feedback and evaluation in English. Have students interview each other about what they learned. Encourage suggestions for ways to improve.

TIME MANAGEMENT IN PROJECT WORK

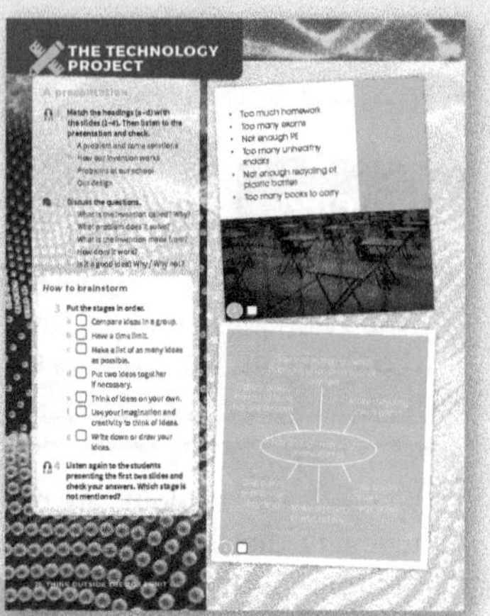

① Be prepared

Take a look at the project before you start the unit.

② Divide the project into smaller tasks

Every project is made of a number of smaller tasks, such as research, preparation, organising notes and brainstorming. Ask yourself:

- *How long will each task take?*
- *Can the task be done in class or out of class?*
- *At what stage of the unit can students complete each step?*
- *What language do they need?*

By approaching the project this way, you will see that the steps may not take up too much class time.

③ Prioritise and set short-term goals

Think about how the project groups can best use class time. Should they brainstorm, draw pictures or organise sentences? Be clear about what you want the groups to achieve by the end of each session.

④ Help students plan out-of-class assignments

Ensure the groups understand that the out-of-class tasks are just as important as the in-class ones when preparing a project. Set goals and give time limits. Encourage them to use their My time-management plans when you see this icon: ⏰

> My time-management plan p71

⑤ Be flexible between projects

How much time you give students for each task will vary from project to project. It may depend on factors such as previous knowledge, level of language difficulty or access to information.

⑥ Set a time for the presentation

Make sure you allow sufficient class time for the presentation step, including its evaluation. If the steps leading to the final product have been distributed and completed in an organised way, it's likely there will be more time for presenting it.

It is important that groups present their projects when they expect to do so. It can be demotivating if you run out of time before they present.

CHALLENGES AND IMPLICATIONS

By Level 3, most students will have shown which combination of learning styles they prefer: visual, aural, verbal, physical or logical. Some will also enjoy learning in groups ('social' learners) while others want to work alone ('independent' learners). The different stages of the project process allow students to develop their learning skills in all of these different ways. You can take advantage of these opportunities throughout the year.

Your third-year students will be part of established social circles, but many will still be going through some emotional and physiological changes. During this year, students' thoughts will also turn towards life after secondary school.

What are some changes and challenges to expect?

Change	Challenge
Academic: more workload and responsibilities	organising time, planning when to study, doing homework, revising for tests, staying motivated
Environment: different teacher and expectations	getting used to a new way of learning, building trust, understanding different expectations
Social: building friendships and social groups	dealing with peer pressure, solving arguments, maintaining good relations, accepting new students
Self growth: physiological, emotional and moral changes	building self-confidence, understanding others, providing emotional support
Personal: more complex personal issues, new interests	sharing personal problems, maintaining open communication

All these changes and their challenges have implications for how to use project work in your classroom. You can encourage successful collaboration by:

- organising your classes in the same way
- explaining how much guidance you will give (less than previous levels), and detailing your expectations
- giving students choices about the ways in which they can work (using the internet, online programs, library, etc.) to encourage motivation
- observing group dynamics
- organising group work from the start
- making sure no one is alone
- developing different skills through varied ways of working (e.g. reflection, peer-evaluation, listening to others)
- continuing to pay attention to each student.

COLLABORATION

Collaborative skills	Behaviours	Level 3 Projects
Listening actively	Responding to others' work or suggestions	**A presentation:** plan information together; invite questions and opinions
Sharing resources	Helping group members to complete or improve work	**A profile of an artist:** find and share online information; help each other find resources
Sharing tasks	Ensuring all group members have a task and role	**A language fact file:** identify the main tasks and roles; divide the work fairly; set deadlines
Using social skills	Giving opinions, persuading, compromising, agreeing	**A report:** agree on content; express opinions politely; ask questions
Encouraging responsibility	Completing tasks on time to finish a project together	**A magazine article:** participate creatively; prepare own section; check each other's work
Disagreeing appropriately	Giving opinions politely to come to a solution	**A presentation:** listen to different points of view; come to a consensus
Giving constructive feedback	Commenting on group members' work	**A travel blog:** make positive comments about and suggest improvements to each other's work
Solving arguments	Reaching a compromise and making final decisions	**A school brochure:** change ideas; listen respectfully
Peer-tutoring	Correcting and editing each other's work	**A poster:** give opinions; make suggestions for changes

Roles and responsibilities

Each project has specific roles, however, here are some general roles that you can apply at any time.

The **group leader** supervises, communicates with the teacher and manages participation.

The **resource manager** looks after resources and keeps the final product for presentation.

The **diary keeper** records decisions and tracks roles and responsibilities.

The **coordinator** tracks time and makes sure individuals complete their tasks.

The **inspector** checks and edits information.

The flipped classroom

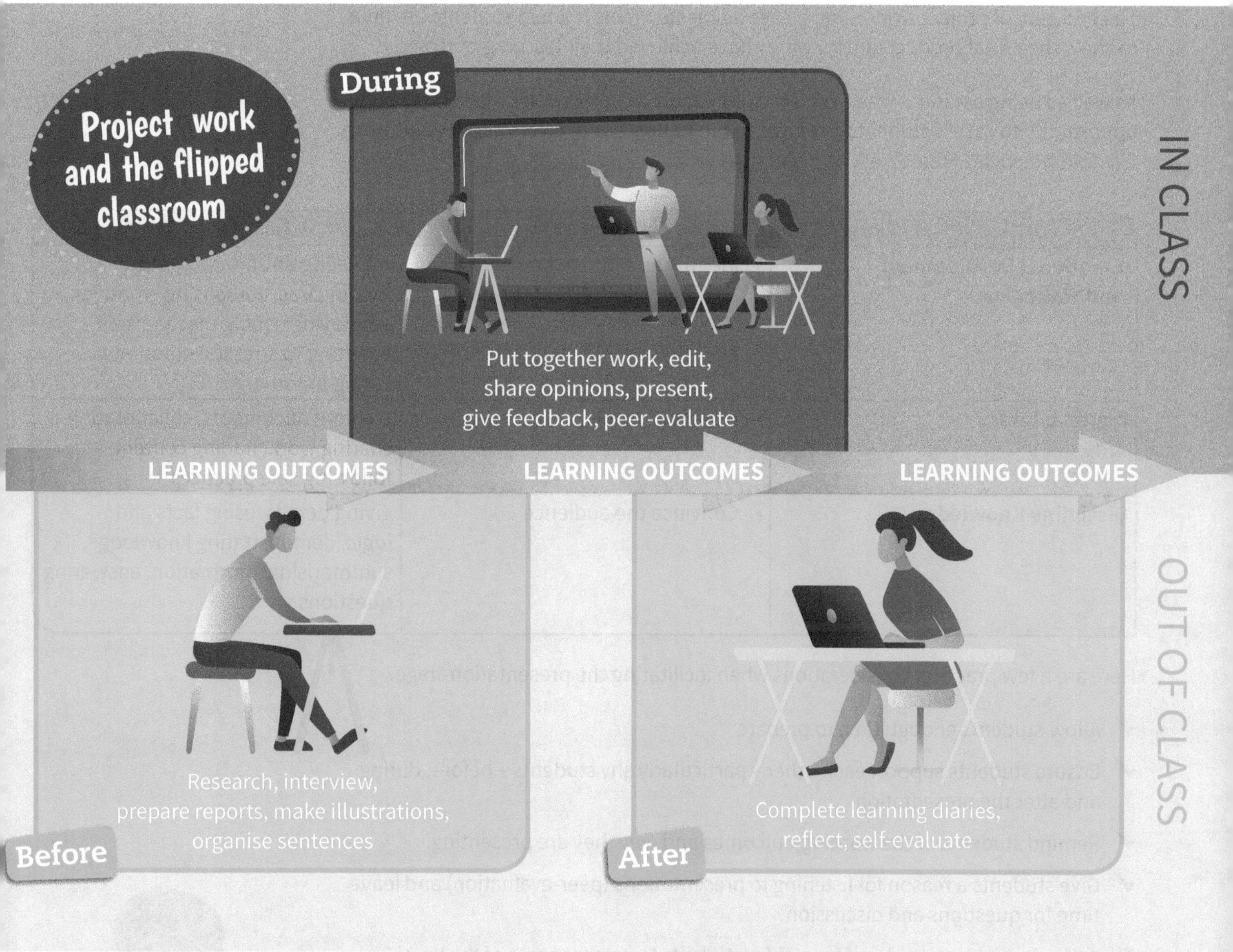

Each project in this book contains at least one flipped classroom idea. Students are still collaborating when they use this approach. They have to share roles, get things ready on time, share information and resources and check one another's work. Students should plan out-of-class project work and use their My time-management plans. > My time-management plan p71

How well did I collaborate?

At the end of the process, have students answer a few questions about how well they collaborated.

Did I ...
help my group?
share information?
do the tasks for my role?

Was I motivated?

Did we ...
trust each other in my group?
share opinions in my group?
share materials in my group?

What can I do to be a better group member?

PRESENTATION IDEAS

The end goal of project work is the presentation step. This is when students are able to show their final product and how they have achieved their learning outcomes.

As well as being a natural way to end the project process, this stage also gives you an opportunity to assess students' progress in the foundational layers of the Cambridge Life Competencies Framework. > Cambridge Life Competencies Framework p6

FOUNDATION LAYERS	ABILITIES	EXAMPLE ACTIONS
Emotional Development and Wellbeing	• Identify and understand emotions • Manage emotions • Empathise and build relationships	reflecting on strengths and weaknesses, verbalising emotions, employing coping mechanisms, adapting to stressful emotions, caring for others
Digital Literacy	• Use digital tools	creating documents, collaborating, sharing work, finding content, following safe practices
Discipline Knowledge	• Convince the audience	giving details, using facts and logic, demonstrating knowledge, summarising information, answering questions

Here are a few practical considerations when facilitating the presentation stage.

✓ Allow students enough time to prepare.

✓ Ensure students support each other – particularly shy students – before, during and after the presentation.

✓ Remind students of the learning outcomes and *why* they are presenting.

✓ Give students a reason for listening to presentations (peer-evaluation) and leave time for questions and discussion.

The following page gives ideas for ways for students to present some of the Level 3 projects. However, they are only suggestions. Where possible, let students choose modes of presentation that are most suitable for their projects and the classroom context.

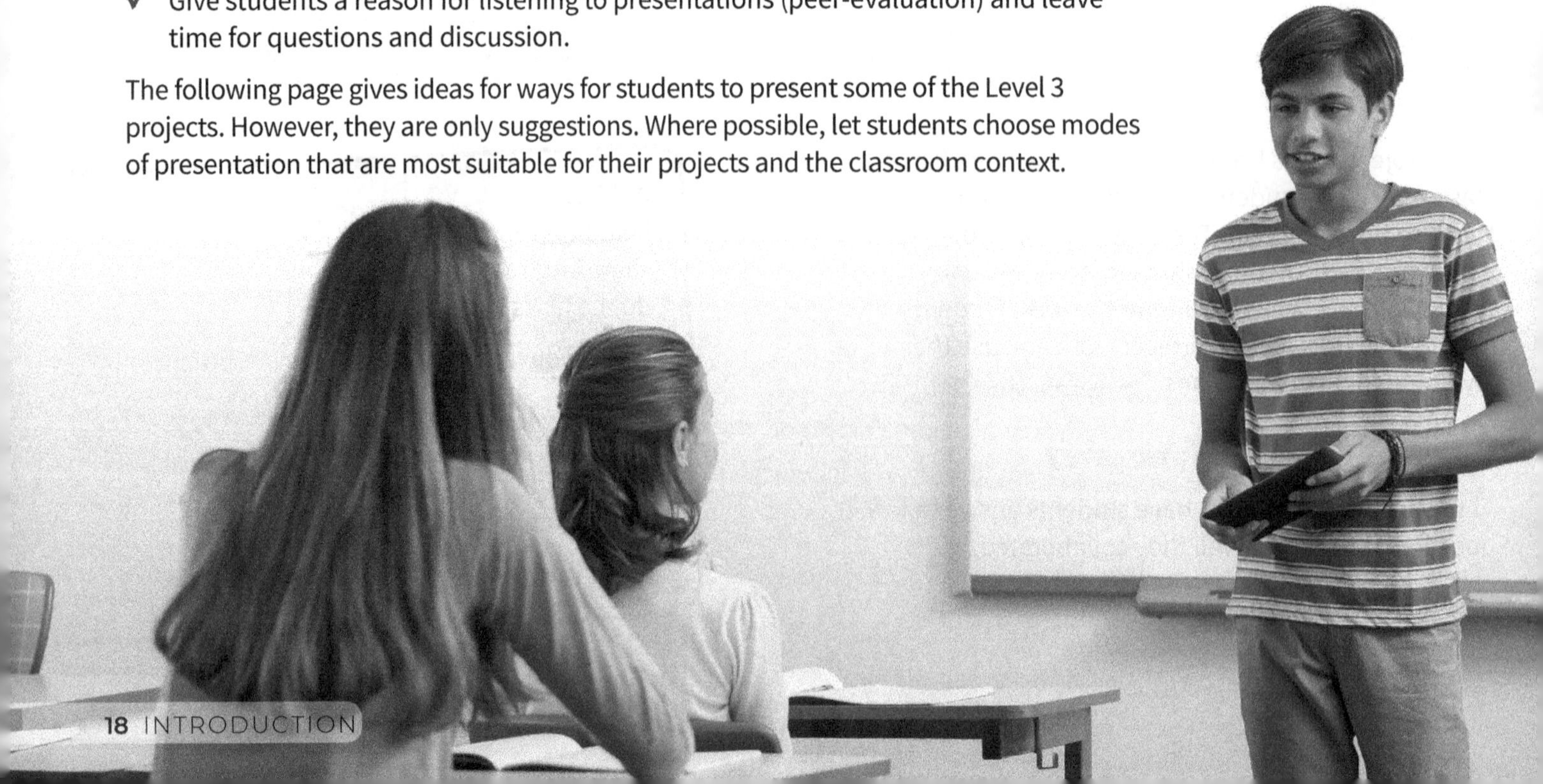

1 PowerPoints

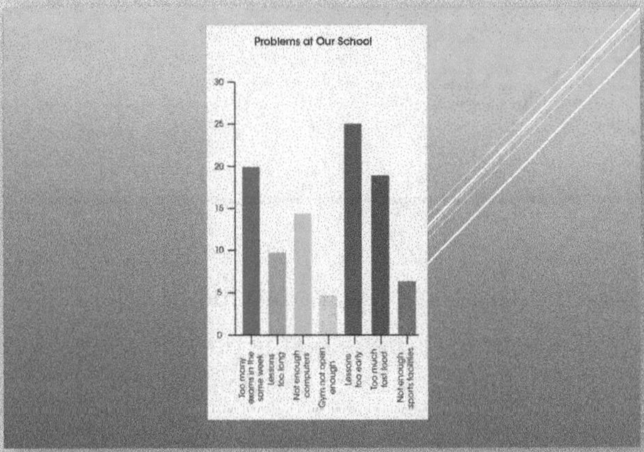

1. **Open the program and click on new presentation**
2. **Choose a design template for each slide**
3. **Add text**
   (click in the box 'click to add text')
4. **Add pictures or diagrams**
5. **Adjust the size of texts, pictures and diagrams**
6. **Check the presentation**
   (correct and edit final version)

2 Timelines

1. **Research** the topic and select events to include.
2. **Look** at different examples of timelines. Choose one and decide how to present events.
3. **Select** your start and end dates. Choose time frames (decades, years, months, etc.).

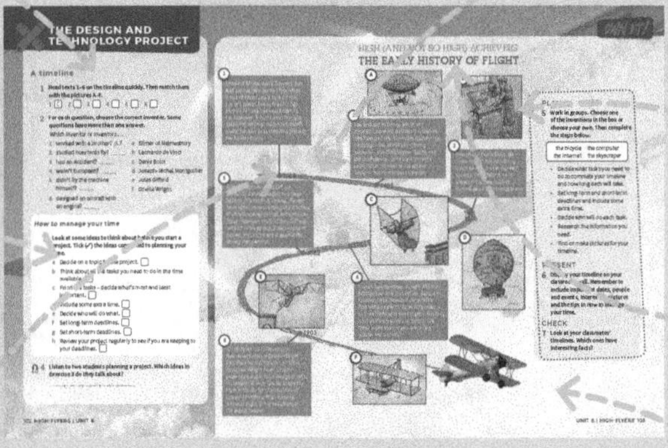

4. **Draw** your timeline.
5. **Add** important details about each event and pictures.
6. **Give** the timeline a title.
7. **Check** the timeline is clear.

Have students use word-processing programs to make timelines or adverts online.

3 Adverts

1. **Look at** a variety of adverts and how they are designed.
2. **Choose** a simple message for your advert.
3. **Write** a memorable title or tagline (what is the advert about).
4. **Add** a few important details.
5. **Include** an attractive picture.
6. **Show** your advert to the class.

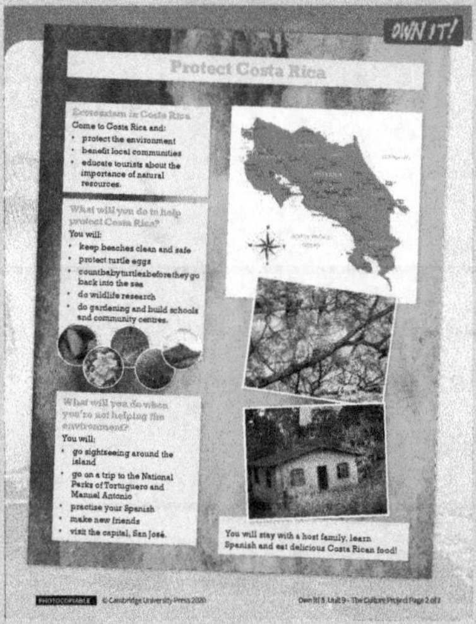

EVALUATION

What?

Product

How well did students achieve their **learning outcomes**?

How well did they demonstrate these?

How did they **evaluate options** and make **decisions**?

Process

How well did students **plan** the product?

How well did students **develop** the project (roles and responsibilities, research and analysis)?

Did students develop **life competencies**?

Who?

Self-evaluation

Peer-evaluation

Teacher–student evaluation

When?

Preparation

After groups are formed: checking learning outcomes, brainstorming ideas, identifying key information, making decisions about content

Development

After each step: thinking about roles and responsibilities, researching and analysing findings, drafting and reviewing

Production

Before presentation: deciding on how to present

During presentation: practising presentation skills

After: giving feedback and self-evaluating

How?

Informal evaluation tools

KWL chart, My learning diary, Peer-evaluation form

> Evaluation tools pp67–69

Formal evaluation tools

Project evaluation rubrics, evaluation rubric, teacher's evaluation form

> Evaluation rubric p21

> Teacher's evaluation form p70

EVALUATION RUBRIC

The rubric below covers areas you can evaluate in every project. You can select some or all of these for each project when you feel it is necessary. There are also two project-specific rubrics with adapted evaluation descriptors in each unit.

Exceeds expectations (4): students show they are ready to go further and can take extra challenges in certain areas.

Very good (3): students complete the tasks successfully and as expected.

Good (2): students complete the tasks reasonably well with some things done better than others.

Needs improvement (1): students show room for improvement in most areas evaluated.

	4	3	2	1
Learning outcomes	Completes all stages to successfully achieve the overall learning outcomes.	Completes most stages effectively. Largely achieves overall learning outcomes.	Has missed some stages. Partially completes overall learning outcomes.	Hasn't successfully completed any of the stages. Overall learning outcomes unachieved.
Planning and organisation	Product is well organised, interesting and easy to follow. It follows the model for the project and no details are missing.	Product is well organised and easy to follow. Some details are incorrect or missing.	Product is similar to the model for the project, but is missing important information. It follows the model with difficulty.	Product does not look or sound anything like the one specified in the task. There is little or no sequence to ideas.
Use of information and resources	Uses a wide range of resources to get information about the product.	Uses different resources to get information, with some gaps.	Most information is relevant and useful, but only comes from one or two resources.	There is little evidence of research and hasn't used appropriate resources.
Collaboration (Teamwork)	Collaborated in all stages and understood roles and responsibilities.	Collaborated in all stages and understood responsibilities. There was minor confusion about roles and responsibilities.	Collaborated in most stages, but there was some confusion about roles and responsibilities.	There was little or no collaboration throughout all stages. Didn't recognise roles and responsibilities.
Time management	Completed everything on time. Revised and corrected project.	Completed everything on time, with one or two steps at the last minute. Revised and corrected project.	Completed all steps, but at the last minute. There was little time for revision or correction.	Did not finish project. Missed steps in the process.
Creativity	Product is very original and interesting. All ideas are well developed.	Product is interesting and very creative. Most ideas are well developed.	There is some evidence of creativity which could have been developed. Product is a mixture of original and copied ideas.	Little creativity. Most ideas copied and pasted from other sources.
Problem-solving skills	All group members participate and listen actively to solve problems at all times.	Most group members are actively involved to solve most problems.	Some evidence of problem-solving but not by all group members.	Little or no evidence of problem-solving, either individually or in groups.
Language use	Excellent use of language. Project is clear and understandable with only a few mistakes.	Good use of language. Project is clear and understandable with some mistakes.	Adequate use of language. Project is understandable, but some sections need further explanation.	Random words are used in a confusing way. Project is almost impossible to understand.
Presentation skills	All group members participate. Presentation is well put-together and is clear and interesting throughout.	All group members participate. Presentation is mostly clear and interesting.	All group members participate, but the method of presentation is sometimes inappropriate or not engaging.	None of the group members fully participate. Inappropriate and uninteresting method of presentation.
Final product	Extremely good.	Very good.	Good.	Needs improvement.

1 THE CULTURE PROJECT

A PRESENTATION

- **Learning outcome:** give a presentation
- **Skills:** research community problems, share material, make notes about problems and solutions, prepare and give a presentation
- **Resources:** two or more video presentations, Presentation organiser p58, My time-management plan p71
- **Evaluation tools:** Project evaluation rubric p25, My learning diary p68, Peer-evaluation form p69, Teacher's evaluation form p70

Unit 1

Before you start
Find two or three different examples of presentations to show students in class. If possible, find video presentations of a speaker giving a talk.

1 Preparation

Step 1: Introduce the topic

- Introduce the topic of presentation any time after doing the vocabulary and the listening activities. p14
- Show students the video presentations. Ask: *What is the topic of each presentation? What information does the presenter give? Who would be interested in this type of presentation?* Focus on some of the techniques the presenter uses: looking at the audience, speaking clearly, etc.
- Explain that a presentation is a way of communicating a message in a speaking situation. It involves presenting information to a group using clear, step-by-step points with visual aids.
- Ask students to find an example of a short presentation online (preferably in English) and bring it to the next class. Tell them to look for a presentation on community problems and possible solutions. Have them look at the presentations in groups and discuss how successful they are. (If the sample presentations are in students' own language, ask questions about it in English and encourage students to explain its content in English.)

Step 2: Analyse the model for the project Unit 1

- Have students read the titles and the information in the problem-solution box. Ask: *Who is Kelvin Doe? Where is he from? Do you think these are good solutions to the problems?* Discuss ideas.
- Have students read the presentation and ask for their opinions. *Do you think this is a good presentation? Who introduces the talk? Who finishes it? What does each presenter talk about? Are the points well developed? Would you change anything?*
- Have students find examples of different **past tense** forms in the presentation. Ask if the problems and solutions are presented in a clear order.

Critical Thinking
Evaluating ideas, arguments and opinions
Monitor students during the class discussion in Step 2 and encourage them to give reasons for agreeing or disagreeing with the ideas in the presentation: *I agree/disagree with what Matt/Adela says because …*

Step 3: *How to* give a presentation Unit 1

- Go through the *How to* tips with the class. Have different students say why each tip is important.
- Ask students how giving a presentation makes them feel. Ask: *Which of the tips will help you feel relaxed and confident when giving a presentation?* Discuss ideas.
- Tell students that when they give their presentations, they should use the tips in this *How to* section.

Step 4: Clarify the project Unit 1

- Follow the steps in > The learning stages of project work p10.
- Brainstorm different problems from your country and write a list on the board.
- Have groups discuss possible solutions for each problem. Then, have the class share ideas.

> My learning diary p68 **Preparation**

> Peer-evaluation form p69 **Preparation**

2 Development

Start this stage as soon as the groups know their learning outcomes and have discussed problems and solutions in their country.

Step 1: Assign roles and responsibilities

- In project groups, have students give each other general roles. > Roles and responsibilities p16 Help them decide on further roles they can share, such as:

The **researcher** checks facts and details about problems and solutions.

The **picture manager** helps choose the images.

The **content organiser** checks the information is correct for each section of the presentation.

The **editor** checks group members' notes.

The **coach** listens to group members' talks and makes suggestions for improvement.

Step 2: Research and analyse Unit 1 p71

- Have groups do the first part of the PLAN section from **Exercise 1**. Have them choose a problem to focus on and brainstorm further problems.

Flipped classroom activity

Out of class: have students research information about the problems. Tell them to check news articles and find evidence from other sources that support arguments. Remind students to look for images.

In class: have students compare their findings in their groups. Ask: *What solutions are there to these problems?* Have students share ideas. Hand out a copy of the > Presentation organiser p58 to each student.

Out of class: have students make notes in the first part of the Presentation organiser at home.

Step 3: Draft and review Unit 1 p71

- Have group members compare their notes on their organisers. Encourage discussion of the ideas and have them choose what to focus on.
- Make sure groups give sections to each member to present.

Flipped classroom activity

Out of class: have students complete the second part of the organiser at home. Tell them to find more detailed information related to the problem and solution they are working on. Tell students that they can write a script for their section if they prefer. However, they should list the most important points to use as notes.

In class: have group members check their work and select images.

Communication
Managing conversations

Monitor progress of the tasks in Steps 2 and 3, checking that all group members are participating and making suggestions for improvements.

Own it! learning tip

Listening actively

When groups are sharing opinions about the information on their organiser, check they are listening to each other's ideas and asking questions to clarify information or get more details. Monitor to help with useful language and invite questions and opinions: *What do you mean? Can you repeat that? Can you explain?* Make sure students show interest and respond respectfully to suggestions on their work.

> My learning diary p68 **Development**

> Peer-evaluation form p69 **Development**

3 Production

Schedule presentation times and stick to them, asking all groups to give their presentations. Spread the presentations over a few lessons, if necessary. Allow enough time for each presentation and for questions.

Allow groups time to work on the visual parts of their presentations. They may wish to create slides on a program such as PowerPoint. > Presentation ideas p19

As students complete their projects, check their abilities in the following Areas of Competency.

Critical Thinking
Evaluating ideas, arguments and options

Analyses causes and effects of problems.

Evidence: Students research the background of each problem and find causes and effects.

Examines possible solutions to a given problem and states how successful they are.

Evidence: Students research a variety of solutions to their problem before choosing the most appropriate (and giving reasons for their choice).

Communication
Managing conversations

Uses appropriate strategies to deal with language gaps (using non-linguistic means, synonyms, etc.).

Evidence: Students give fluent presentations without reading directly from notes.

Invites contributions from interlocuters in a conversation.

Evidence: Groups ask for and answer questions from the class at the end of their presentations.

Step 1: Prepare Unit 1 p71

- Go through the PRESENT section from **Exercise 2**. Remind students that each group member will present their problems and solutions.
- Encourage students to give feedback as they make final changes to their presentations. Help with language, particularly use of appropriate register and different **past tenses**.
- Monitor to check that the problems and solutions are presented in a clear way. Ask students how the images they chose help their presentations and how they are going to present them.
- Remind groups of the presentation date and how much time each group will have.
- Allow groups time to practise their presentations. Refer them to the tips in the *How to* box.

Step 2: Present Unit 1

- Draw attention to the CHECK section from **Exercise 3**. Ask the class to think about these questions as they listen to their presentations.
- Have groups give their presentations. Tell the class to make notes as they listen.
- Allow two or three minutes for questions at the end of each presentation.

Step 3: Reflect Unit 1

- After the presentations, hold a class discussion on the CHECK questions in **Exercise 3**.
- Have students vote on the most interesting presentation and say why. Tell students to pay particular attention to different groups' analysis of problems and solutions. (See Differentiated instruction activities below for further practice.)

Differentiated instruction

Support
Have students choose their favourite presentation and make a problem-solution chart, similar to the table on the second page.
Consolidation
Have students write their presentation in the form of a magazine article. Tell them to use all of their groups' ideas on the organisers.
Extension
Have students choose their favourite presentation and make an informative poster with charts and images that describe the problems and solutions.

- Encourage students to think about each stage of the project process, including positive experiences and things they could improve. Ask: *How well did you work in your group? Did you give feedback as you were practising the presentations? Did you follow the tips in the 'How to' box? What was difficult about presenting?*

> Peer-evaluation form p69 **Production and Reflection**

Go to the digital collaboration space to set, track and assess students' work, or allow students to share and comment on their own work.

Project evaluation rubric: a presentation

Use these project-specific descriptors and your own choice of descriptors from the > Evaluation rubric on p21 to check students individually or in groups. Make your own evaluation form. > Teacher's evaluation form p70

	4	3	2	1
Creativity	Product provides an excellent analysis of problems. It contains many creative and interesting solutions. It is supported by clear, attractive and meaningful images. It is easy to understand.	Product provides a good analysis of problems. It contains some creative and interesting solutions. It is supported by mostly clear, attractive images. It is logical and fairly easy to understand.	Product provides some analysis of problems. It contains solutions, but they are not very creative or interesting. It is supported by images, although some are not clear. It is difficult to understand in parts.	Product does not provide analysis of problems. It does not contain any solutions. It doesn't have images. It is illogical and impossible to understand.
Presentation skills	Speaks slowly, clearly and looks at the audience. Remembers what to say and uses notes well. Keeps very good time. Asks for questions and answers them all with confidence.	Speaks slowly, clearly and looks at the audience most of the time. Remembers what to say most of the time, but reads from script occasionally. Keeps good time. Asks for questions and answers most of them clearly.	Speaks slowly, clearly and looks at the audience some of the time. Forgets some things and reads from script quite often. Is slightly too slow or fast. Answers some questions, but doesn't ask for any.	Doesn't speak slowly or clearly and doesn't look at the audience. Reads everything from a script. Is much too slow or fast. Doesn't ask for or answer questions.

Cambridge Life Competencies Framework

You can also check students' progress in the following foundation layers.

FOUNDATION LAYERS	ABILITIES	ACTIONS
Emotional Development and Wellbeing	• Manage emotions	giving constructive feedback, listening actively, managing conversations, providing support and confidence, adapting to stressful situations (presenting)
Discipline Knowledge	• Convince the audience	presenting ideas, analysing problems and solutions, summarising information, giving details, describing images, answering questions

Flipped classroom activities

Evaluate

In project groups, have students discuss their completed Peer-evaluation forms and ways to work better as a group. > Peer-evaluation form p69

Out of class: Have students think about their progress at home. > My learning diary p68 **Production**

In class: Hold a class discussion on what students have learned, using the information from their learning diaries. Ask: *How confident do you feel presenting in front of groups? What can you do to increase your confidence?*

> My learning diary p68 **Production**

A PROFILE OF AN ARTIST

- **Learning outcome:** make a profile of an artist
- **Skills:** conduct online research, find pictures, make notes about an artist, combine information and pictures to make a profile
- **Resources:** examples of magazine profiles, Profile organiser p59, My time-management plan p71
- **Evaluation tools:** Project evaluation rubric p29, KWL chart p67, Peer-evaluation form p69, Teacher's evaluation form p70

Student's Book pp30–31

Before you start

Find two or three examples of profiles of artists in magazines or online. Check the examples give some or all of the information in the categories on p30.

1 Preparation

Step 1: Introduce the topic

- Introduce the topic of profiles after doing the reading exercises. p24
- Show students the examples of the profiles. Discuss who they are about and what kind of information they would expect to read about them. Ask: *What information can you see? Are there any images? Who would want to read these profiles? Where can you find them?*
- Explain that a profile is information that usually focuses on a person and what is important or interesting about them. This might include information about their personal and professional lives. Tell students that profiles can be about anyone: they don't have to be famous.
- Ask students to bring an example of a profile (in English) to the next lesson. Divide the class into groups to discuss which profiles they find most interesting and why.

Step 2: Analyse the model for the project pp30–31

- Complete **Exercises 1** and **2**. Look at the pictures and have students describe what they can see. Ask: *Who is Ben Heine? Do you like his art? Why/Why not?* Have students make notes.

Answers 1 Students' own answers. 2 Nationality: Belgian; Education: painting and sculpture at art college in the UK; Interests: photography, playing music, languages; Types of art: combines illustration and photography; Exhibitions: in Africa, Asia, Europe, the USA.

- Ask questions about the effectiveness of the model profile. For example: *Does the profile contain important and interesting facts about the artist? Is the information well organised? Which information comes first, second, etc.? Which information do you find most interesting? Why?*
- Revise the language from the unit. Ask students to find examples of the **present perfect** in the profile. Ask why the profile uses this tense (to talk about actions, experiences and facts when the exact time is not mentioned and there is a relationship to the present).

Step 3: *How to* do online research p30

- 2.10 Go through the *How to* tips in **Exercise 3** with the class. Discuss possible answers, before playing the audio in **Exercise 4** to check.

Answers 3 a to e are all ways of checking online information; f refers to using online research to create an original piece of work, not just copy.

- Discuss the advice given in the audio. Stress the importance of using a variety of resources to crosscheck information and using educational websites that are intended for students. Tell them to check that information is up to date and remind them not to copy information word for word.

Learning to Learn

Taking control of your own learning

Have students make a note of the ideas in the *How to* conduct online research. Have them think about whether they follow this advice in English and other subjects.

Step 4: Clarify the project pp30–31

- Follow the steps in > The learning stages of project work p10.
- Brainstorm a list of artists with the class. Hold a short discussion on what type of art they produce.
- Have groups discuss ideas about the kind of information readers would like to know about the artists.

> KWL chart p67 **Know and Want to know**

> Peer-evaluation form p69 **Preparation**

2 Development

Start this stage as soon as groups know their learning outcomes and are ready to choose an artist from the list.

Step 1: Assign roles and responsibilities

- In project groups, have students share the general roles. > Roles and responsibilities p16 Help them decide on further roles and responsibilities they can share.
- Explain that there are some important roles and responsibilities when creating a profile. Draw a diagram like this on the board:

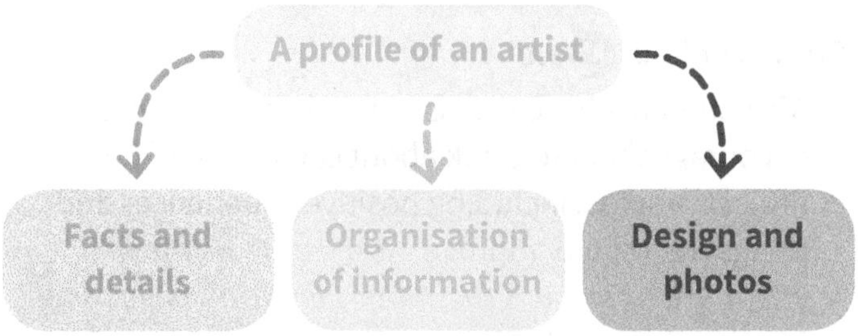

- Discuss the different tasks required to create a profile of an artist.

  Facts and details: *What sources can you use to find information? How can you check the facts are correct? Who will decide on important or interesting details to include?*

  Organisation of information: *How will you divide the profile into sections? What kind of information will go in each section? What supporting details will you include? Who will make the final decisions on the organisation of information?*

  Design and photos: *How will you make the profile attractive? Where can you find images of the artist's work? Do the images match the information in the texts? Who will select the images?*

- Encourage students to take notes and give each other roles and responsibilities.

Step 2: Research and analyse p31 p71

- Allow groups time to discuss which artist they want to write a profile about. Encourage them to give opinions and make arguments for their choice.
- Hand out a copy of the > Profile organiser p59 to each student.

Flipped classroom activity

Out of class: have group members complete the notes in the first part of their organisers as per the first three bullets of the PLAN section in **Exercise 5**. Tell them to conduct their research and find images using different sources.

In class: Have group members check their work together and decide on the most interesting information.

Step 3: Draft and review p31 p71

Flipped classroom activity

Out of class: have groups finish the PLAN section in **Exercise 5**.

In class: Have students check each other's drafts and discuss ideas for combining their information.

Have groups work together to write two questions about their profiles. Explain that these questions should ask for their classmates' opinions or responses to the artist's work.

Creative Thinking

Creating new content from own ideas or other resources

Monitor the conversations in the groups as they put together their project. Check that group members are using a variety of sources before deciding on final content to include.

Own it! learning tip

Sharing resources

Each group member should share useful information (online biographies, photos of the artist, images of his or her work etc.) and details about how and where they found the information.

> Peer-evaluation form p69 **Development**

3 Production

Schedule presentation times and stick to them. The projects can be presented at the same time on the wall, but give enough time for students to look at all the profiles and answer each other's questions.

Before groups produce their final drafts, have them think of creative and attractive ways to present their profiles, such as a poster or timeline. > Presentation ideas p19

As students complete their projects, check their abilities in the following Areas of Competency.

Learning to Learn

Take control of your own learning

Finds sources of information and help (online).

Evidence: Students conduct online research to find and use a variety of sources.

Chooses ways to practise English outside the classroom.

Evidence: Students use English language sources to gather information (online sites, documentaries, etc.).

Creative Thinking

Creating new content from own ideas or other resources

Makes an assignment original by changing the task or adding new angles.

Evidence: Groups choose a creative and attractive way to present their final profiles.

Communicates personal response to creative work from art, music or literature.

Evidence: Students answer the groups' questions about their profiles and give their opinions on the artists' work.

Step 1: Prepare p31 p71

- Go through the PRESENT section in **Exercise 6**.
- As groups prepare their final profiles, ask questions: *Are the facts and dates correct? Have you checked your information? What photos or illustrations are you using? Do the texts match them? Is the design attractive? What can you do to improve it?*
- Check use of the **present perfect** in the texts. Allow enough time for final corrections.
- Remind groups of the presentation date and how much time each group will have.

Step 2: Present p31

- Have groups put their profiles on the classroom walls.
- Draw attention to the CHECK section. Have groups walk around the classroom and look at all of the profiles. Give them time to answer each other's questions.
- Tell students to make notes about each profile, then decide on their favourite in groups. (See Differentiated instruction activities below for further practice.)

Differentiated instruction

Support
Have students vote on the best profile and share the result with the class, giving reasons for their opinions.
Consolidation
Have pairs list the strong and weak things about one of the profiles and share the list with that group.
Extension
In project groups, students write three questions about specific facts regarding their artist. Then have two groups quiz each other.

Step 3: Reflect p31

- After students have discussed their favourite profile, encourage them to think about each stage of the project process, including positive experiences and things they could improve. Ask: *Was it easy to find information on your artist? Is any information missing? Where can you get this missing information?*

> Peer-evaluation form p69 **Production and Reflection**

Go to the digital collaboration space to set, track and assess students' work, or allow students to share and comment on their own work.

Project evaluation rubric: a profile of an artist

Use these project-specific descriptors and your own choice of descriptors from the > Evaluation rubric on p21 to check students individually or in groups. Make your own evaluation form. > Teacher's evaluation form p70

	4	3	2	1
Creativity	Product is very well organised and has a very attractive and creative design. It uses interesting and appropriate images. It contains interesting information, including accurate facts from a variety of sources.	Product is well organised and has an attractive design. It uses appropriate images, and the majority of them are interesting. It has some information, including accurate facts from reliable sources.	Product is fairly well organised and has a clear but not very attractive design. It uses appropriate images, but they are not interesting. It has accurate information from reliable sources, but few facts are relevant.	Product is poorly organised and has an unattractive design. It has very few or no images and none of them are appropriate or interesting. It doesn't have accurate or relevant information.
Language use	Product shows excellent use of language from unit (present perfect). Project is understandable with few or no mistakes.	Product shows good use of language from unit (present perfect). Project is understandable but with some mistakes.	Product shows adequate use of language from unit (present perfect). Project is understandable, but some sections need further explanation.	Product doesn't use language from unit (present perfect). Project is confusing, and almost impossible to understand.

Cambridge Life Competencies Framework

You can also check students' progress in the following foundation layers.

FOUNDATION LAYERS	ABILITIES	ACTIONS
Digital Literacy	• Use digital tools	collaborating, sharing work, finding content, checking sources, using appropriate and safe sites, attributing sources and creating new content
Discipline Knowledge	• Convince the audience	explaining facts and images, giving details, summarising information, asking and answering questions, giving biographical information

Flipped classroom activities

Evaluate

In project groups, have students discuss their completed Peer-evaluation forms and ways to work better as a group. > Peer-evaluation form p69

Out of class: Have students think about their progress at home. > KWL chart p67 **Learned**

In class: Hold a class discussion on what students learned, using the information from their KWL charts. Ask: *Do you want to find out more about any of the artists? Why/Why not?* Hold a short discussion.

> KWL chart p67 **Learned**

3 THE CULTURE PROJECT

A LANGUAGE FACT FILE

- **Learning outcome:** make a language fact file
- **Skills:** decide on categories and visual elements for fact files, find information for each category, if possible record a video or audio
- **Resources:** two or more fact files, Language fact file organiser p60, My time-management plan p71
- **Evaluation tools:** Project evaluation rubric p33, My learning diary p68, Peer-evaluation form p69, Teacher's evaluation form p70

Unit 3

Before you start
Collect two or three different fact files to show students in class.

1 Preparation

Step 1: Introduce the topic

- Introduce the topic of fact files after doing the vocabulary exercises. p35
- Show students the fact files. Ask them to say what they are for and where we can find them.
Ask: *What are fact files about? Why do people read them? Have you ever read a fact file? What was it about? Why did you read it?*
- Explain that fact files usually present information on a single page in tables or lists. They focus on key points about a topic and can include statistics. Ask: *What topics can fact files be about? (They can give information about a place, person, event or product).*
- Ask students to bring a fact file (in English) to the next class. Have them discuss which fact files are interesting or successful and why.

Step 2: Analyse the model for the project Unit 3

Flipped classroom activity

Out of class: have students read the fact file model and think of one more part to add.

In class: ask questions about the fact file: *How does it present the information? What is the main topic? What statistics are there? Have you learned anything new?*

Have students compare the model fact file with the examples they brought to class.

Learning to Learn
Practical skills for participating in learning
Check the homework in Step 2. Write students' categories on the board.

Step 3: *How to* make a fact file Unit 3

- Go through the ideas with the class. Students discuss which categories they can include, which formats they can use (paper or digital) and where to find information and images. They also brainstorm ideas for recording video or audio and/or for sources where they could find recorded material.
- Check students understand that when they make their fact files, they should use the ideas in the *How to* section.

Step 4: Clarify the project Unit 3

- Follow the steps in > The learning stages of project work p10
- Brainstorm different countries and their languages. Write a list on the board.
- Have groups choose a country and language for their fact file.
- If groups are presenting digitally, ask them what programs they can use. Brainstorm ideas.

> My learning diary p68 **Preparation**

> Peer-evaluation form p69 **Preparation**

2 Development

Start this stage as soon as groups know their learning outcomes and have chosen their country, language and format for presenting their fact file.

Step 1: Assign roles and responsibilities

- In project groups, have students decide on general roles. > Roles and responsibilities p16 Help them decide on further roles they can share, such as:

The **graphic designer** decides on fonts, sections and layout.

The **picture manager** finds appropriate and accurate maps.

The **editor** makes the final decision on what content to include.

The **digital editor** creates the digital version and embeds video or audio.

The **fact checker** checks content details.

Flipped classroom activities

Step 2: Research and analyse Unit 3 p71

Out of class: have groups research information for each of the categories in their fact file. Set a time for when they should start organising their notes in class.

Step 3: Draft and review Unit 3 p71

In class: hand out a copy of the > Language fact file organiser p60 to each student to help them plan their information.

Have groups do the PLAN section from **Exercise 1**. Give them time to share information and make notes.

Group members decide who prepares each section.

Out of class: group members prepare their sections.

In class: group members check each other's sections and put their fact file together.

Collaboration
Managing the sharing of tasks in a project

Monitor progress of the tasks in Step 3 to check group members are making decisions together.

Own it! learning tip

Sharing tasks

Have group members monitor each other's progress and their ability to complete their tasks on time. Help them solve problems and encourage them to come to agreements about schedules and roles. For example: *I can do the …, Sorry, I won't be able to …, Can I be the … ?*

> My learning diary p68 **Development**

> Peer-evaluation form p69 **Development**

3 Production

Schedule presentation times and stick to them, checking that all groups present their fact files. Spread the presentations over a few classes, if necessary. Allow enough time for each presentation and for questions.

Before groups produce their final drafts, have them decide on the format for presenting their fact file, if they haven't done so yet. It could be a digital presentation with video and/or audio or a print poster.

> Presentation ideas p19

As students complete their projects, check their abilities in the following Areas of Competency.

Learning to Learn
Practical skills for participating in learning

Completes homework as required.

Evidence: Students are ready to do the work planned for the in-class project session.

Takes effective notes in class and from homework reading.

Evidence: Fact file contains relevant information from various sources.

Collaboration
Managing the sharing of tasks in a project

Participates with others to plan, organise and carry out events.

Evidence: Group members complete their tasks with help from others.

Ensures that work is fairly divided among members in group activities.

Evidence: Group members divide responsibilities and make decisions together.

Step 1: Prepare Unit 3 p71

- Go through the PRESENT section in **Exercise 2**.
- As groups prepare their project, ask questions: *Did you check your facts? Have you included maps and photos? Is your fact file a digital presentation or a poster?* Give enough time for final adjustments.
- Remind groups of the presentation date and how much time each group will have.
- Encourage groups to practise and time their presentation. (See Differentiated instruction activities below for further practice.)

Differentiated instruction

Support
Give group members extra time to practise their part of the presentation and give them tips on how to improve.
Consolidation
Encourage group members to listen actively to each other while they are practising and to give positive feedback.
Extension
Have group members manage how tasks are shared and who should present which sections. Tell them to focus on individual students' interests.

Step 2: Present Unit 3

- Draw attention to the CHECK section from **Exercise 3**. Ask the class to think about these questions as they listen to each other's presentations.
- Have groups present their fact files. Remind speakers to take their time and speak clearly.
- Remind students to speak clearly and ask for questions at the end of each section or of the whole presentation.

Step 3: Reflect Unit 3

- After all the presentations, hold a class discussion on the CHECK questions in **Exercise 3**.
- Encourage students to think about each stage of the project process, including positive experiences and things they could improve.

> Peer-evaluation form p69 **Production and Reflection**

Go to the digital collaboration space to set, track and assess students' work, or allow students to share and comment on their own work.

Project evaluation rubric: a language fact file

Use these project-specific descriptors and your choice of descriptors from the > Evaluation rubric p21 to check students individually or in groups. Make your own evaluation form. > Teacher's evaluation form p70

	4	3	2	1
Creativity	Product has a good design and good use of maps, photos and drawings. It contains common phrases and a wide range of interesting facts. It uses a wide variety of digital or print resources.	Product has nice design with good use of maps, photos and drawings. It contains some common phrases and interesting facts. It uses some digital or print resources.	Product has a basic design with some use of maps, photos and drawings. It contains a few common phrases and ordinary facts. It uses a few digital or print resources.	Product has an unattractive design. It contains no common phrases and no interesting facts. It uses only one digital or print resource.
Use of information and resources	Uses interesting and correct information. Presents information in appropriate categories.	Uses interesting and mostly correct information. Presents most information in appropriate categories.	Uses interesting information, but some of it is incorrect. Presents some information in the wrong categories.	Uses incorrect information. Presents all information in an illogical way.

Cambridge Life Competencies Framework

You can also check students' progress in the following foundation layers.

FOUNDATION LAYERS	ABILITIES	ACTIONS
Digital Literacy	• Use digital tools	finding content on various online sources, checking facts with other digital sources, using digital tools to design and present the fact file
Discipline Knowledge	• Convince the audience	giving details, researching and checking facts, demonstrating knowledge by answering questions, taking effective notes

Flipped classroom activities

Evaluate

In project groups, have students discuss their completed Peer-evaluation forms and ways to work better as a group. > Peer-evaluation form p69

Out of class: Have students think about their progress at home. > My learning diary p68 **Production**

In class: Hold a class discussion on what students have learned, using the information from their learning diaries.

> My learning diary p68 **Production**

4 THE PE PROJECT

A REPORT

- **Learning outcome:** write a report about your school
- **Skills:** write yes/no questions, interview classmates, identify and write solutions, prepare a report, present results
- **Resources:** two or more reports about school and health, Report organiser p61, My time-management plan p71
- **Evaluation tools:** Project evaluation rubric p37, KWL chart p67, Peer-evaluation form p69, Teacher's evaluation form p70

Student's Book pp54–55

Before you start

Collect two or three different reports about health-related issues at school to show students in class.

1 Preparation

Step 1: Introduce the topic

- Introduce the topic of reports after completing the vocabulary exercises. p47
- Show students the reports. Ask questions about each one: *What is this report about? What question(s) does it ask and answer? What are the results? How does the writer present the results? What does the writer think?*
- Explain that people write reports for a clear purpose. It presents and then studies information related to a particular problem or issue. Ask: *Have you written reports in other subjects? What kind of topics can reports be about?* Write a list on the board.
- Ask students to bring an example of a report related to school issues (preferably in English) to the next lesson. Have students discuss the reports, identifying the purpose, problems, results/solutions and conclusions.

Step 2: Analyse the model for the project pp54–55

- Discuss the questions in **Exercise 1** with the class. Brainstorm ideas for how schools can help.
- Have students read the report and do **Exercise 2**. Check their predictions from **Exercise 1**.

Answers 2 1 f 2 a 3 d 4 c 5 b 6 e.

- Ask questions about the effectiveness of the report: *Is the purpose clear? Does the report find the problems and give solutions? What pictures do the writers use? Do they help? Why/Why not?*
- Revise the language from the unit. Ask students to find and circle examples of **quantifiers *(too many/much, a little, a few*** and ***(not) enough)*** and **modals *should, shouldn't*** and ***ought to*** for advice.

Critical Thinking

Evaluating ideas, arguments and opinions

As students think about the project model, have them discuss which suggestions they think are most realistic or useful and give reasons for their ideas.

Step 3: *How to* do a survey p54

- Go through the tips in **Exercise 3**. Hold a class discussion about which ideas students agree with and encourage them to give reasons for their ideas.

Answers 3 a, c, d and e are good tips (for e, they can ask for extra information regarding solutions).

- Have the class write up a list of essential tips to use when they do a survey, using their answers from **Exercise 3**. Ensure students understand that when they write their reports, they should use these tips.

Step 4: Clarify the project pp54–55

- Follow the steps in > The learning stages of project work p10. Point out that for this project, students will work in pairs.
- Go over the list of ideas for how schools can help students be healthier. Have pairs add to the list.

> KWL chart p67 **Know and Want to know**

> Peer-evaluation form p69 **Preparation**

2 Development

Start this stage as soon as pairs know their learning outcomes and have a list of ideas of how schools can help students be healthier.

Step 1: Assign roles and responsibilities

- Have students share the general roles. Remind them that as they are working in pairs they will need to take on more responsibilities than if they were in a group. > Roles and responsibilities p16 Help them decide on further roles and responsibilities they can share.
- Explain that there are some important roles when writing a report. Draw a diagram like this on the board:

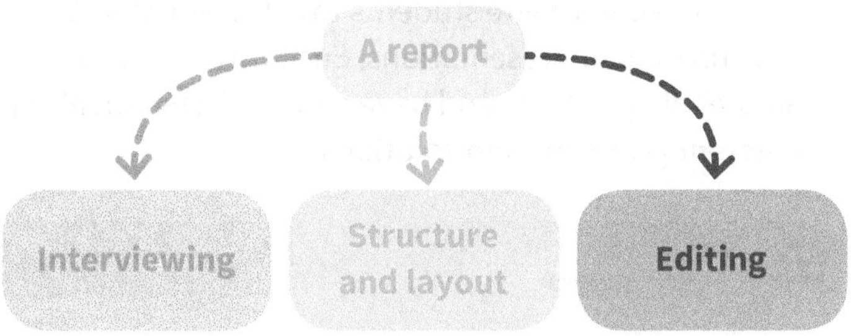

- Discuss the different tasks required to write a report.

  Interviewing: *Do you have a list of useful questions for your report? When and where will you do your survey? Who will ask the questions? Who will record the answers? How will you record the answers?*

  Structure and layout: *What information goes in the introduction? What sections will the report have? How will you present problems and solutions? How will you present the results? Who will be responsible for the design?*

  Editing: *Is the report easy to understand? Are the problems and solutions clear? Is all of the information clear? Who is responsible for final content?*

- Encourage students to take notes and share roles and responsibilities.

Step 2: Research and analyse p55 p71

- Hand out a copy of the > Report organiser p61 to each student and have them read the first part of the PLAN section in **Exercise 4**. Tell them to complete the Purpose and Questions section of the organiser in their pairs. Have them use their ideas and the ideas in the box.
- Remind students to use language and vocabulary from the unit in the questions.
- Have pairs interview their classmates. Tell them to record the answers in their notebooks and highlight problems that their classmates mention. Remind students to introduce themselves, ask questions and say thank you when they finish.

Communication
Managing conversations

Monitor students as they conduct their interviews and check that they are asking and answering all of the questions.

Flipped classroom activity

Out of class: have students complete the rest of their organisers. Tell them to think about their classmates' answers and put together a list of problems in their organiser. Then, have them complete the organiser with their own ideas and solutions. Point out that this includes their own ideas to solve the problems and ideas for presenting the information.

In class: have pairs compare the information in their organisers and decide on what to include in their reports. (See Differentiated instruction activities below for further practice.)

Differentiated instruction

Support
Help pairs decide on final content by finding out which of their ideas are most useful for the report.
Consolidation
Allow pairs time to read the solutions on each other's organisers and decide a final list of ideas.
Extension
Encourage pairs to discuss what to include in their final reports and give arguments for and against each solution.

Step 3: Draft and review p55 p71

- Have students put their final ideas onto paper to draft their reports. Remind them to separate their information into clear sections.
- Encourage discussion about how to present their ideas.

> Peer-evaluation form p69 **Development**

3 Production

Schedule presentation times and stick to them, checking all pairs present their reports. Spread the presentations over a few classes, if necessary. Allow time for each presentation and for questions.

Allow pairs time to work on the visual elements for their presentations. They may wish to create slides on a program such as PowerPoint. > Presentation ideas p19

As students complete their projects, check their abilities in the following Areas of Competency.

Critical Thinking
Evaluating ideas, arguments and options

Gives reasons for an argument's plausibility.

Evidence: Report has a clear purpose in relation to how schools can help students be healthier and identifies problems and solutions.

Assesses strengths and weaknesses of possible solutions.

Evidence: Pairs select the best solutions after discussing strengths and weaknesses.

Communication
Managing conversations

Uses appropriate language to negotiate meaning (seek repetition, check understanding).

Evidence: Answers all questions in classmates' surveys and checks information when necessary.

Uses simple techniques to start, maintain and close conversations of various lengths.

Evidence: Pairs conduct surveys by introducing themselves, asking questions and saying thank you.

Step 1: Prepare p55 p71

- Go through the PRESENT section from **Exercise 5**.
- As pairs prepare their final reports, ask questions. For example: *How are you dividing your sections? What are the problems? Do you have a solution for each problem? What language are you using for giving advice?*
- Tell pairs that they must decide who will present which part of their report. Suggest that they take turns presenting problems and solutions.
- Remind pairs of the presentation date and how much time each pair will have.

Step 2: Present p55

- Draw attention to the CHECK section from **Exercise 6**. Ask the class to think about the questions as they listen to the presentations.
- Have groups show their reports and give their presentations. Tell the class to make notes about each report and write questions they want to ask.
- Make sure pairs invite students to ask questions at the end of their presentations. Encourage pairs to answer all questions and have a class discussion about different problems and solutions.

Own it! learning tip

Using social skills

As pairs present and discuss their reports in Step 2, remind them to use polite language for introducing themselves and their work, asking questions and saying thank you: *Our report is about ..., We'd like to present some information about ..., Does anyone have any questions?, Thank you for listening.*

Step 3: Reflect p55

- After the presentations, hold a class discussion on the questions in the CHECK section in **Exercise 6**.
- Write positive opinions about each report on the board. Then have the class vote for the best idea.
- Encourage students to think about each stage of the project process, including positive experiences and things they could improve.

> Peer-evaluation form p69 **Production and Reflection**

Go to the digital collaboration space to set, track and assess students' work, or allow students to share and comment on their own work.

Project evaluation rubric: a report

Use these project-specific descriptors and your own choice of descriptors from the > Evaluation rubric p21 to think about students individually or in pairs. Make your own evaluation form. > Teacher's evaluation form p70

	4	3	2	1
Creativity	Product is very well organised with clear questions and language. It discusses lots of problems and gives very creative solutions. It uses attractive and easy-to-follow pictures.	Product is well organised with mostly clear questions and simple language. It discusses some problems and gives some creative solutions. It uses easy-to-follow pictures.	Product has fairly clear questions and simple language, but is sometimes difficult to follow. It discusses one or two problems and gives solutions, although they are not very creative. It uses pictures that are difficult to follow.	Product is not well organised and is impossible to follow. It doesn't discuss problems or give solutions. It doesn't have pictures.
Language use	Product shows excellent use of grammar, punctuation and spelling. It shows excellent use of language from unit (quantifiers and modals for giving advice). Project communicates its main ideas clearly with few or no mistakes.	Product shows good use of grammar, punctuation and spelling. It shows good use of language from unit (quantifiers and modals for giving advice). Project communicates its main ideas clearly but with some mistakes.	Product shows adequate use of grammar, punctuation and spelling. It shows adequate use of language from unit (quantifiers and modals for giving advice). Project communicates some of its ideas clearly, but some sections need further explanation.	Product shows poor use of grammar, punctuation and spelling. It doesn't use language from unit (quantifiers and modals for giving advice). Project is confusing and almost impossible to understand.

Cambridge Life Competencies Framework

You can also check students' progress in the following foundation layers.

FOUNDATION LAYERS	ABILITIES	ACTIONS
Emotional Development and Wellbeing	• Empathise and build relationships	asking and answering questions politely, listening attentively, making decisions in pairs, thanking people for taking part and listening, giving positive feedback
Discipline Knowledge	• Convince the audience	using simple language, identifying problems and providing creative solutions, analysing and presenting results, organising structure of a report

Flipped classroom activities

Evaluate

In project groups, have students discuss their completed Peer-evaluation forms and ways to work better as a group. > Peer-evaluation form p69

Out of class: Have students think about their progress at home. > KWL chart p67 **Learned**

In class: Hold a class discussion on what students have learned, using the information from their KWL charts. Ask: *Do you think reports are an effective way of presenting information? How else could you present the information from your survey?*

> KWL chart p67 **Learned**

A MAGAZINE ARTICLE

- **Learning outcome:** write a magazine article
- **Skills:** find information about a tribal nation, organise information in a spidergram, divide work into paragraphs, add photos, maps and drawings
- **Resources:** two or more magazine articles, Magazine article organiser p62, My time-management plan p71
- **Evaluation tools:** Project evaluation rubric p41, My learning diary p68, Peer-evaluation form p69, Teacher's evaluation form p70

Unit 5

Before you start
Collect two or three different magazine articles about different tribal nations to show students in class. Choose articles that give a variety of information in English, supported by images.

1 Preparation

Step 1: Introduce the topic

- Introduce the topic of magazine articles after doing the reading exercises. p60 Ask: *Do you know any interesting magazines? What are they about? Why do people read magazine articles?*
- Show students the magazine articles. Ask: *What are these articles about? What type of magazine are they from? How is the information organised? Would you want to read these articles? Why/Why not?* Discuss which articles students like the most and why.
- Explain that magazine articles give details about events, people or places and focus on topics that are of interest to the reader.
- Ask students to bring an example of a magazine article in English to the next lesson. Have them talk about the topic of each article and who would read it.

Step 2: Analyse the model for the project Unit 5

Flipped classroom activity

Out of class: have students read the model magazine article and think about these questions: *Which tribe is the article about? What information does the title give? What is the topic of each paragraph? Is there a problem? If so, what is it? Why?*

In class: have students discuss their ideas.

Ask students to find similarities and differences between the model magazine article and the examples brought to class.

Social Responsibilities
Understanding personal responsibilities as part of a group and in society

Ask students about the Nenets' way of life and what they have to do individually and as a group.

Step 3: *How to* write a magazine article Unit 5

- Go through the *How to* tips with the class. Ask students to look at the model again and find the things described in the tips. Ask: *What kind of information goes in each paragraph?*
- Tell students that before they present their articles, they should check that they have followed the tips in this *How to* section.

Step 4: Clarify the project Unit 5

- Follow the steps in > The learning stages of project work p10.
- Have groups discuss how they can find out more information about different tribal nations. Encourage them to do some research and brainstorm a list in the next class.

> My learning diary p68 **Preparation**

> Peer-evaluation form p69 **Preparation**

2 Development

Start this stage as soon as groups know their learning outcomes and have brainstormed a list of different tribal nations.

Step 1: Assign roles and responsibilities

- In project groups, have students decide on general roles. > Roles and responsibilities p16 Help them decide on further roles they can share, such as:

The **editor** checks titles and paragraph structure and checks no content is missing.

The **proof reader** checks grammar, spelling and punctuation.

The **graphic designer** thinks about the design of the article.

The **fact checker** checks content details.

The **picture manager** chooses the images.

Step 2: Research and analyse Unit 5 p71

- Have students start the PLAN section from **Exercise 1**. Discuss which of the tribal nations from the brainstormed list are suffering from climate change. If there is time, have students research information. Tell groups to choose a tribal nation to write about.
- Have groups discuss which key words will help them find information about their tribal nation and write a list.
- Hand out a copy of the > Magazine article organiser p62 to each student.

Creative Thinking

Participating in creative activities

Monitor how well group members participate in Steps 2 and 3. Encourage them to be creative when thinking about the results of different situations.

Flipped classroom activity

Out of class: have students complete the spidergram in the first part of their organiser. Encourage them to use the internet to search for information and to use the key words they discussed with their groups.

In class: have group members compare their information. Tell them to organise their notes in the second part of the organiser. Ask groups: *What is the biggest problem your tribal nation faces?* and use their answers to help with ideas for a title and general introduction. Encourage groups to add as many notes as possible, using the ideas in the PLAN section. Give time for them to do more research in class or at home. Have group members decide who will prepare each section.

Step 3: Draft and review Unit 5 p71

Flipped classroom activity

Out of class: have students work on their sections. Remind them to check their grammar, spelling and punctuation and to find images for their text.

Tell students to try to include examples of first and second conditionals to talk about possible situations that result from the problems described.

In class: have group members check each other's work. Tell them to check content and language. Then, have groups put their work together to make a first draft.

Own it! learning tip

Encouraging responsibility

Tell students it is important to complete their sections on time so that their groups can finish the project in class. Remind group members of their general roles, including participating creatively, preparing their own sections and checking each other's work. Discuss any problems groups may be having in keeping to schedule. Discuss why this is happening and encourage or suggest possible solutions.

> My learning diary p68 **Development**

> Peer-evaluation form p69 **Development**

3 Production

Schedule presentation times and stick to them, so each group can present their articles. Spread the presentations over a few lessons, if necessary. Allow enough time for each presentation and for questions.

Before groups produce their final drafts, talk about how they will present their information. They may wish to present their article digitally, for example on PowerPoint.

> Presentation ideas p19

As students prepare and present their projects, check their abilities in the following Areas of Competency.

Social Responsibilities

Understanding personal responsibilities as part of a group and in society

Understands the rights and responsibilities of individuals in society at local and national levels.

Evidence: Students discuss tribal nations' rights and responsibilities in relation to climate change.

Understands various aspects of society.

Evidence: Group members research different ways of life and understand how societies differ and why.

Creative Thinking

Participating in creative activities

Encourages group members to make activities more original and imaginative.

Evidence: Groups find interesting information about their tribal nation from a variety of sources.

Participates in 'what if' thinking.

Evidence: Students discuss possibilities as a result of different situations.

Step 1: Prepare Unit 5 p71

- Go through the PRESENT section in **Exercise 2**.
- As groups prepare their project, encourage students to check each other's work and give feedback. (See Differentiated instruction activities box for further practice.)
- Say that each group member will present their section. If the group is presenting on PowerPoint or another digital program, make sure they assign one group member the role of technician. Give students time to practise their parts in their groups.
- Remind groups of the presentation date and how much time each group will have.

Differentiated instruction

Support
Help students with self- and peer-correction. Check their work and point out areas that need improvement.
Consolidation
Encourage students to use different resources (websites, dictionaries) to check facts, language and spelling.
Extension
Let students make final decisions over corrections on content and language. Encourage them to explain their reasons to the group.

Step 2: Present Unit 5

- Draw attention to the CHECK section in **Exercise 3**. Ask the class to make notes about the items on the checklist as they listen to their peers' presentations.
- Have groups present their articles. Remind speakers to look at their audience and ask for questions at the end of their presentation.

Step 3: Reflect Unit 5

- After all the presentations, hold a class discussion on what they like about each article, before they vote on their favourite.
- Ask: *Was planning/researching/designing your article easy/difficult? Why/Why not?*
- Encourage students to think about each stage of the project process, including positive experiences and things they could improve.

> Peer-evaluation form p69 **Production and Reflection**

Go to the digital collaboration space to set, track and assess students' work, or allow students to share and comment on their own work.

Project evaluation rubric: a magazine article

Use these project-specific descriptors and your own choice of descriptors from the > Evaluation rubric p21 to check students individually or in groups. Make your own evaluation form. > Teacher's evaluation form p70

	4	3	2	1
Creativity	Product is very well researched with lots of information about a tribal nation. It has an interesting and appropriate title. It uses attractive photos, maps and drawings. It shows very creative 'what if' thinking.	Product is well researched with a good amount of information about a tribal nation. It has an appropriate title. It uses fairly attractive photos, maps and drawings. It shows some creative 'what if' thinking.	Product is well researched in parts with some information about a tribal nation. It has a title that is only a little bit about the content. It uses one or two photos, maps and drawings. It doesn't show much creative 'what if' thinking.	Product is not well researched and has no interesting information about a tribal nation. It has a title but it isn't about the content. It doesn't use photos, maps and drawings. It doesn't show any creative 'what if' thinking.
Language use	Product shows excellent use of grammar, punctuation and spelling. It shows excellent use of language from the unit (first and second conditionals). Project communicates its main ideas clearly with few or no mistakes.	Product shows good use of grammar, punctuation and spelling. It shows good use of language from the unit (first and second conditionals). Project communicates its main ideas clearly but with some mistakes.	Product shows adequate use of grammar, punctuation and spelling. It shows adequate use of language from the unit (first and second conditionals). Project communicates some of its ideas clearly.	Product shows poor use of grammar, punctuation and spelling. It doesn't use language from the unit (first and second conditionals). Project is confusing and almost impossible to understand.

Cambridge Life Competencies Framework

You can also check students' progress in the following foundation layers.

FOUNDATION LAYERS	ABILITIES	ACTIONS
Emotional Development and Wellbeing	• Empathise and build relationships	sharing creative and original ideas, discussing possible solutions to problems, understanding different cultures
Discipline Knowledge	• Convince the audience	giving details, supporting ideas with evidence, explaining facts and images, demonstrating knowledge of tribal nations and their problems, answering questions

Flipped classroom activities

Evaluate

In project groups, have students discuss their completed Peer-evaluation forms and ways to work better as a group. > Peer-evaluation form p69

Out of class: Have students think about their progress at home. > My learning diary p68 **Production**

In class: Hold a class discussion on what have students learned, using the information from their learning diaries. Ask: *What new things did you learn about tribal nations around the world?*

> My learning diary p68 **Production**

6 THE TECHNOLOGY PROJECT

A PRESENTATION

- **Learning outcome:** present an idea for an invention
- **Skills:** brainstorm ideas, choose solutions, draw ideas, design an invention, make slides
- **Resources:** two or more ideas for inventions, Invention organiser p63, My time-management plan p71
- **Evaluation tools:** Project evaluation rubric p45, KWL chart p67, Peer-evaluation form p69, Teacher's evaluation form p70

Student's Book pp78–79

Before you start
Find two or three inventions online. If possible, bring pictures of the inventions, along with details of what they are for and why they are good ideas.

1 Preparation

Step 1: Introduce the topic

- Continue with the topic of inventions after doing the reading exercises. p72
- Show students the inventions you found. Have them discuss what the inventions are for. Ask: *What do you think of these inventions? What problem(s) do they solve? Are they useful? Why/Why not?*
- Explain that an invention can use technology to solve specific problems. Say that in the design of an invention, the inventors need to show how the invention works, as well as what it is for. Ask for examples of famous or useful inventions and write a list on the board.
- Have students bring details of an invention to the next lesson. Discuss the purpose of each invention and whether students think it is a good idea or not.

Step 2: Analyse the model for the project pp78–79

- 6.12 Have students complete **Exercise 1**. Play the audio for students to check their answers.

Answers 1 1 c 2 a 3 d 4 b.

- Use the questions in **Exercise 2** to discuss the invention. When students discuss if they think the invention is a good idea, ask: *Is the purpose of the invention clear? Does it solve the problems on the students' list? Is the design clear and simple?*

Answers 2 1 Recycling sounds; it's a musical recycling machine 2 Not enough recycling of plastic bottles 3 Metal and glass 4 When a student recycles a plastic bottle, they can listen to a song and they collect points to win a prize. 5 Students' own answers.

- If there is time, play the audio again and have students call out when they hear examples of the **passive**.

Step 3: *How to* brainstorm p78

- Go through the stages in **Exercise 3**. Have students work in pairs to put them in order and then check answers with the class.

Answers 3 The correct order is b, e, a, c, f, d.

- 6.13 Play the first half of the audio (the first two slides) again. Have students check off the items on the *How to* list and say which one is missing. Point out that illustrating ideas is the final step in the process, after brainstorming and discussing all the problems and solutions.

Answers 4 g.

Collaboration
Working towards a resolution related to a task
Have students identify steps in the brainstorming process where they work together and share ideas. Ask: *Why is it important to share ideas when brainstorming?* and discuss ideas.

Step 4: Clarify the project pp78–79

- Follow the steps in The learning stages of project work p10. Explain to students that they are going to present an idea for an invention. For this project, have them work in groups of four.
- Draw attention to the model again. Tell students they will make a PowerPoint presentation of their invention idea.

KWL chart p67 **Know and Want to know**

Peer-evaluation form p69 **Preparation**

2 Development

Start this stage as soon as groups know their learning outcomes.

Step 1: Assign roles and responsibilities

- In project groups, have students share the general roles > Roles and responsibilities p16. Help them decide on further roles and responsibilities they can share.
- Explain that there are some other important roles and responsibilities when presenting an idea for an invention. Draw a diagram like this on the board:

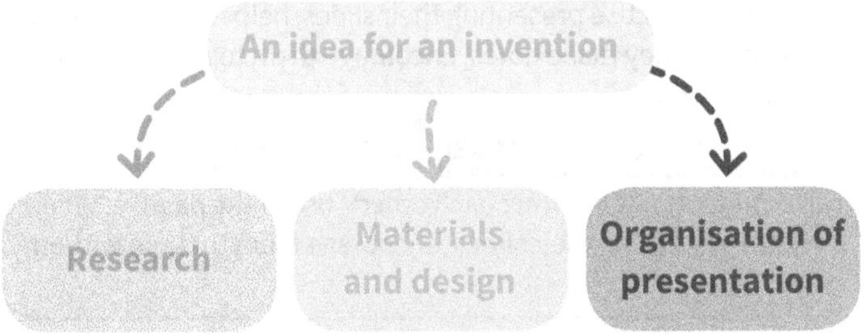

- Discuss the different tasks for presenting an idea for an invention.

  Research: *What ideas do you have for solving the problems? How will they work? What can you use to help you? Who will make the final decisions on the best ideas to use?*

  Materials and design: *What are the best materials to use for your invention? What design will your invention have? Is it simple or complicated? Is it clear how the invention works? Who will decide on the final design?*

  Organisation of presentation: *How many slides will you have? What information is on each slide? Is the presentation easy to follow? Who will present each slide? Who will make the slides?*

- Encourage students to take notes and share roles and responsibilities.

Step 2: Research and analyse p79 p71

- Have groups start the PLAN section in **Exercise 5**. Hand out a copy of the > Invention organiser p63 to each student.
- Remind students of the ideas in the *How to* box when listing problems, comparing ideas, choosing problems and thinking of solutions.

Flipped classroom activity

Out of class: have students make a list of problems using their organisers.

In class: have groups brainstorm solutions together, and complete the spidergram in the second part of their organisers. Monitor to check students are being creative and thinking of original and crazy ideas.

Out of class: have students complete parts 3 and 4 of their organisers at home. Remind them that they should label materials and describe how their invention works.

Step 3: Draft and review p79 p71

- Have students compare their invention ideas in their groups. Give them time to discuss the strengths and weaknesses of each idea and then decide on the final design.
- Tell groups to draft four slides for their presentation. Encourage them to prepare one slide each and tell them they will each present the slide they work on.
- Encourage group members to review each other's slides and suggest improvements. Have them work together in class to make final slides for their presentation or share roles for group members to prepare parts of the presentation at home.

Communication

Participating with appropriate confidence and clarity

Monitor progress of the tasks in Step 3 to check how well students link their ideas on each slide into a presentation.

Own it! learning tip

Disagreeing appropriately

If students cannot agree on which ideas to include in their inventions, encourage polite discussion and ask them to give their opinions explaining their reasons. Have them make alternative suggestions to come to a solution all group members agree with. Give them some useful language, for example:
I'm not sure about ..., I don't agree because ..., Why don't we...?, How about ... ?, Maybe we should ...

> Peer-evaluation form p69 **Development**

3 Production

Schedule presentation times and stick to them, so that all groups can present their inventions. Spread the presentations over a few lessons, if necessary. Allow enough time for each presentation and for questions.

Offer help and suggest ideas for how groups can make the slides for their PowerPoint presentations.

> Presentation ideas p19

As students complete their projects, check their abilities in the following Areas of Competency.

Collaboration

Working towards a resolution related to a task

Is aware others have divergent views and ideas for solving a task.

Evidence: Students listen and work together to make final decisions on what ideas to include in their inventions.

Is able to propose solutions that include other views and ideas from their own.

Evidence: Students use the ideas from their organisers to create new solutions.

Communication

Participating with appropriate confidence and clarity

Develops a clear description or narrative with a logical sequence of points.

Evidence: Final presentation slides are clear with information presented in a logical order.

Uses a number of cohesive devices to link sentences into a clear, coherent discourse.

Evidence: Students use clear language for describing processes (passive).

Step 1: Prepare p79 p71

- Go through the PRESENT section in **Exercise 6**.
- Allow time for groups to practise presenting their slides. Monitor to check students are using language for describing their inventions and processes (**passive**). Help them with vocabulary for materials. (See Differentiated instruction activities box for further practice.)
- Tell groups to double check that their slides are not missing any details and that information is presented in the correct order.
- Remind groups of the presentation date and how much time each group will have.

Differentiated instruction

Support
As students practise presenting their slides, help them make passive sentences. Allow them to make and use notes as they need to.
Consolidation
As students practise presenting their slides, help them use passive sentences. If they make notes, encourage them to refer to them as little as possible.
Extension
Have students peer-correct each other's use of the passive. When they are presenting their slides, encourage them to do so without notes.

Step 2: Present p79

- Draw attention to the CHECK section in **Exercise 7**. Ask the class to consider which items from the checklist each group covers as they listen to the presentations.
- Have groups present their inventions. Remind students to each present the slide they worked on. Tell speakers to look at their audience.
- Tell the class to make notes of good ideas and things that they think won't work, and to say why.
- Encourage the class to ask questions at the end of each presentation.

Step 3: Reflect p79

- After the presentations, hold a class discussion on the CHECK questions in **Exercise 7**.
- Encourage students to think about each stage of the project process, including positive experiences and things they could improve. Ask: *Did you collaborate and communicate effectively when preparing your project? Why/Why not?*

> Peer-evaluation form p69 **Production and Reflection**

Go to the digital collaboration space to set, track and assess students' work, or allow students to share and comment on their own work.

Project evaluation rubric: a presentation

Use these project-specific descriptors and your own choice of descriptors from the > Evaluation rubric p21 to check students individually or in groups. Make your own evaluation form. > Teacher's evaluation form p70

	4	3	2	1
Creativity	Product is very creative with lots of original ideas for how an invention works. It clearly solves a problem in an imaginative way. It has a large list of solutions. Everyone communicates well.	Product is creative with some original ideas for how an invention works. It solves a problem in a fairly imaginative way. It uses a list of solutions. Most people communicate well.	Product is quite creative with one or two original ideas for how an invention works. It solves a problem but not very imaginatively. It uses a small list of solutions. One or two group members communicate.	Product is not creative with no original ideas for how an invention works. It does not solve a problem and is not imaginative. It doesn't use list of solutions. Group members did not communicate well.
Language use	Presentation shows excellent use of language from the unit (passive). Project communicates its main ideas clearly with only a few mistakes.	Presentation shows good use of language from the unit (passive). Project communicates its main ideas clearly but with some mistakes.	Presentation shows adequate use of language from the unit (passive). Project communicates some of its ideas clearly, but some sections need further explanation.	Presentation doesn't use language from the unit (passive). Project is confusing and almost impossible to understand.

Cambridge Life Competencies Framework

You can also check students' progress in the following foundation layers.

FOUNDATION LAYERS	ABILITIES	ACTIONS
Emotional Development and Wellbeing	• Identify and understand emotions	making decisions together, disagreeing appropriately, looking at the audience, adapting to stressful emotions (talking in front of a large group)
Digital Literacy	• Use digital tools	working collaboratively on slides, using programs for making a presentation (PowerPoint), combining digital information with oral presentation

Flipped classroom activities

Evaluate

In project groups, have students discuss their completed Peer-evaluation forms and ways to work better as a group. > Peer-evaluation form p69

Out of class: Have students think about their progress at home. > KWL chart p67 **Learned**

In class: Hold a class discussion on what students have learned, using the information from their KWL charts. Ask: *How did you feel when you presented your slides?* Discuss ways to feel more confident in future (be well prepared, practise more, use body language, etc.).

> KWL chart p67 **Learned**

A TRAVEL BLOG

- **Learning outcome:** write a travel blog
- **Skills:** research information about a festival, organise information in a spidergram, create a title, write in the first person, find maps, photos and drawings, prepare a section of a blog
- **Resources:** two or more travel blogs about festivals, Travel blog organiser p64, My time-management plan p71
- **Evaluation tools:** Project evaluation rubric p49, My learning diary p68, Peer-evaluation form p69, Teacher's evaluation form p70

Unit 7

Before you start
Look at different travel blogs online. Find examples of blogs about visits to festivals. Choose two or three to show students in class.

1 Preparation

Step 1: Introduce the topic

- Introduce the topic of travel blogs after doing the vocabulary exercises. p83 Ask: *What kinds of texts do people use to share their travel experiences? What type of information do they have?* Share ideas.
- Show students the travel blog examples. Ask: *Which festivals are they about? When and where do they take place? What do people do there? Why do you think these festivals are important?* Have students share ideas.
- Explain that a blog is a type of website, usually by one person, that presents information in a conversational style. Ask students if they read any blogs and why. Ask: *What topics are blogs about?* Have students share examples.
- Ask students to find a blog about a festival around the world. Have them discuss in groups the content and design of the blogs.

Step 2: Analyse the model for the project Unit 7

- Have students look at the title and pictures in the model blog. Ask: *Which festival is this blog about? Where is the festival? What happens at this festival?* Have students read the blog and check.
- Ask: *When did the festival begin? How often does it take place? What is special about the festival? What activities are there to do? How does the writer feel about the festival?*
- Ask questions about the blog's design and purpose: *Is the blog attractive? Who would read it? Is the language of the blog formal or informal? Are you interested in visiting the festival? Why/Why not?* (See Differentiated instruction activities below for further practice.)

Differentiated instruction

Support
Have students work in pairs. Ask them to make multiple-choice questions about the blog and test another pair.
Consolidation
Have students work in pairs. Have them choose one of the photos in the blog and write a description of what they can see and how it makes them feel.
Extension
Tell students to imagine they are visiting the festival. Have them agree on three things they are going to do and make a plan.

Social Responsibilities
Understanding and describing own and others' cultures

As students look at the model, have them discuss why the festival is important. Ask: *Are there any similar festivals in our country?* and compare cultures.

Step 3: *How to* write a blog Unit 7

- Go through the *How to* tips with the class. Have different students say why each tip is important.
- Check students understand that when they write their blogs, they should use the tips in this *How to* section.

Step 4: Clarify the project Unit 7

- Follow the steps in The learning stages of project work p10.
- Brainstorm a list of festivals from around the world. Write ideas on the board.

My learning diary p68 **Preparation**

Peer-evaluation form p69 **Preparation**

2 Development

Start this stage as soon as groups know their learning outcomes and have brainstormed a list of festivals.

Step 1: Assign roles and responsibilities

- In project groups, have students share roles Roles and responsibilities p16. Help them decide on further roles they can share, such as:

The **editor** checks all the text and graphics are present.

The **proof reader** checks grammar, spelling and punctuation.

The **graphic designer** controls the design of the blog.

The **fact checker** checks content details.

The **picture manager** chooses the images.

Step 2: Research and analyse Unit 7 p71

- Have groups start the PLAN section from **Exercise 1**. After they agree which festival to write about, give a copy of the Tavel blog organiser p64 to each student.

Flipped classroom activity

Out of class: have group make notes in the spidergram on their organisers. Tell them to find as much information as they can.

In class: have group members compare notes and think of a title. Tell them to decide which sections to prepare. Encourage groups to look at the types of section that travel blogs contain. Ask them what new section they can include.

Step 3: Draft and review Unit 7 p71

Flipped classroom activity

Out of class: have group members prepare their section of the blog as explained in the PLAN section. Remind students that they should write in the first person as if they visited the festival and that they should use a friendly style. Tell them to research and make more notes in their spidergrams. Tell them to complete the second part of their organisers and find images.

In class: have group members check each other's sections and then make a first draft of their blog. Have groups decide on the final design for their blog. Tell them to decide which images to include.

Out of class: students may want to present their blogs digitally. If so, have groups work on the design and share and correct their work online. Have them use free online blog templates.

Creative Thinking

Using newly created content to solve problems and make decisions

Make sure all students discuss what to include in their final blogs. Encourage them to be creative with their final design and the sections they include.

Own it! learning tip

Giving constructive feedback

As students look at each other's work in Steps 2 and 3, encourage them to make suggestions for how sections could be improved. Help with useful language. For example:

I like ..., This is good because ... , That is really clear ..., I like it, but why don't you ... ?, Why don't we ...?, That's a good idea, but ..., What about ...?

My learning diary p68 **Development**

Peer-evaluation form p69 **Development**

3 Production

Schedule presentation times and stick to them, so that all groups can present their blog posts. Spread the presentations over a few lessons, if necessary. Allow time for each presentation and for questions.

Offer help and suggest ideas for how groups can complete their final versions successfully. If students are presenting digitally, they may want to use PowerPoint, online blog templates or video. > Presentation ideas p19

As students prepare and present their projects, check their abilities in the following Areas of Competency.

Social Responsibilities

Understanding and describing own and others' cultures

Accepts others and shows respect for cultural difference, challenges prejudice and discriminatory views.

Evidence: Groups write about cultural aspects of the festival in their blogs in a positive way.

Makes informed comparisons between their own and other societies.

Evidence: Students compare the festival to their own culture in discussions and writing.

Creative Thinking

Using newly created content to solve problems and make decisions

Employs new ideas and content in solving a task.

Evidence: Blogs contain interesting descriptions and sections presented in a creative way.

Makes an assignment original by changing the task or adding new angles.

Evidence: Presentation contains interesting elements (images, digital, slides, video, etc.).

Step 1: Prepare Unit 7 p71

- Go through the PRESENT section in **Exercise 2**.
- As groups prepare their final project, remind them of the tasks they need to complete and the tips in the *How to* box. Tell them that they should be ready to answer questions, particularly about their own sections.

Flipped classroom activity

Out of class: have students finish their blog entries at home, based on their group's comments. If they are presenting digitally, tell them to share tasks online. Encourage them to try out different fonts and colours to draw attention to their blog (print or digital).

In class: have groups make the final corrections to their blog. Have them focus on content and design before checking grammar, punctuation and spelling.

- Remind groups of the presentation date and how much time each group will have.

Step 2: Present Unit 7

- Draw attention to the CHECK section in **Exercise 3**. Ask the class to think about these questions as they listen to all the presentations.
- If the blog is digital, have groups give one group member the role of technician.
- Have groups present their blogs. Tell students to each present the section they worked on. Remind speakers to look at their audience and ask for questions at the end of their presentation.
- Tell the class to make notes on what they like about each blog and which festival they would like to visit. Encourage them to give reasons for their opinions.

Step 3: Reflect Unit 7

- After the presentations, hold a class discussion on the CHECK questions in **Exercise 3**.
- Have the class discuss what they found interesting about each blog. Then, hold a class vote on which festival they would like to go to. Have them discuss reasons why.
- Encourage students to think about each stage of the project process, including positive experiences and things they could improve. Ask: *Is there any information missing from your blog? How can you make it more interesting?* Talk about the blogs' features as well as content.

> Peer-evaluation form p69 **Production and Reflection**

Go to the digital collaboration space to set, track and assess students' work, or allow students to share and comment on their own work.

Project evaluation rubric: a travel blog

Use these project-specific descriptors and your own choice of descriptors from the > Evaluation rubric p21 to check students individually or in groups. Make your own evaluation form. > Teacher's evaluation form p70

	4	3	2	1
Creativity	Product contains a wide variety of interesting information about a festival. Product has an excellent design and is interesting for the reader. It has an interesting title. It is very well organised and has creative and original sections.	Product contains a variety of interesting information about a festival. Product has a good design and is fairly interesting for the reader. It has a fairly interesting title. It is well organised and has a few creative and original sections.	Product contains one or two pieces of interesting information about a festival. Product contains images, but the content is not very interesting for the reader. It has a title, but it is not interesting. It is organised but not very creative.	Product does not contain any interesting information about a festival. Product does not have any images and is uninteresting for the reader. It has an inappropriate title. It is disorganised and doesn't have any creative sections.
Language use	Shows excellent use of informal language to describe an event. Shows excellent use of grammar, punctuation and spelling. Project communicates its main ideas clearly with only a few mistakes.	Shows good use of informal language to describe an event. Shows good use of grammar, punctuation and spelling. Project communicates its main ideas clearly but with some mistakes.	Shows adequate use of informal language to describe an event. Shows adequate use of grammar, punctuation and spelling. Project communicates some of its ideas clearly, but some sections need further explanation.	Does not use appropriate or informal language to describe an event. Shows poor use of grammar, punctuation and spelling. Project is confusing.

Cambridge Life Competencies Framework

You can also check students' progress in the following foundation layers.

FOUNDATION LAYERS	ABILITIES	ACTIONS
Digital Literacy	• Use digital tools	finding content, checking information, creating a blog, collaborating and sharing work online, using digital presentation techniques, adding interactive features
Discipline Knowledge	• Convince the audience	describing experiences, giving details about festivals, demonstrating knowledge, identifying cultural aspects, answering questions, using appropriate language and register

Flipped classroom activities

Evaluate

In project groups, have students discuss their completed Peer-evaluation forms and ways to work better as a group. > Peer-evaluation form p69

Out of class: Have students think about their progress at home. > My learning diary p68 **Production**

In class: Hold a class discussion on what students have learned, using the information from their learning diaries. Ask: *What makes blogs interesting for readers? Are they a useful source of information? Why/Why not?*

> My learning diary p68 **Production**

A TIMELINE

- **Learning outcome:** design a school brochure
- **Skills:** ask for and make suggestions, discuss pros and cons, find solutions, make decisions
- **Resources:** two or more brochures or website information for schools, Brochure organiser p65, My time-management plan p71
- **Evaluation tools:** KWL chart p67, Peer-evaluation form p69, Teacher's evaluation form p70, Project evaluation rubric p53

Student's Book pp102–103

Before you start

Collect two or three school brochures to show students in class. If this is not possible, find general information pages from school websites.

1 Preparation

Step 1: Introduce the topic

- Introduce the topic of brochures any time after doing the vocabulary activities. p95 Ask: *Where can you find information about schools? How do they advertise? Does our school have a brochure or website? What kind of information is in/on it?* Discuss ideas.
- Show students the brochures or webpages. Encourage them to say what they are for and describe how they designed. Ask: *What sections do the brochures have? What photos do they use? What information do they give?*
- Explain that brochures are a type of information leaflet that introduce an organisation, such as a school or company, and tell the reader about what they do. Point out that many schools now do this online.
- Ask students to bring an example of a brochure or webpage for a school or organisation to the next lesson. Have them discuss the different sections of the brochures and the information they present and find out how the brochure presents a positive image.

Step 2: Analyse the model for the project pp102–103

- Discuss **Exercise 1** with the class. Ask them which section provides the answer ('What makes Unity Hill Unique?').

Answers 1 Students make their own rules.

- Complete **Exercise 2**. Allow students time to read the model carefully and write their opinions. They should think about the rules and responsibilities. Have them discuss ideas in pairs and encourage students to give reasons for their answers.
- Revise the language from the unit. Have students circle examples of ***can***, ***can't***, ***must***, ***mustn't***, ***have to*** and ***don't have to*** and ask them what they are used for.

Collaboration
Listening respectfully and responding constructively to others' contributions

Monitor pairs' discussions and explanations for their ideas. Encourage them to listen and respond to each other. *That's true., What about …?, I think this section is clear., Me too., So do I!, etc.*

Step 3: *How to* make decisions in a group p102

- 8.10 Go through the stages in **Exercise 3** with the class. Have students put the ideas in order and ask them if they follow these stages when making decisions as a group in class. Play the audio to check the order.

Answers 3 The correct order is c, e, f, a, b, d.

- As you check students' answers, ask: *Why is it important for everyone to make decisions together? How can you find the best solution if you disagree about ideas? (Make compromises, make other suggestions, etc.)*

Step 4: Clarify the project pp102–103

- Follow the steps in > The learning stages of project work p10.
- Say: *Imagine your perfect school. What makes it special?* Brainstorm ideas and write the best on the board.

> KWL chart p67 **Know and Want to know**

> Peer-evaluation form p69 **Preparation**

2 Development

Start this stage as soon as groups understand the learning outcomes and have brainstormed a list of ideas for what makes a school special.

Step 1: Assign roles and responsibilities

- In project groups, have students share the general roles > Roles and responsibilities p16. Help them decide on further roles and responsibilities they can share.
- Explain that there are some important roles and responsibilities when creating a brochure. Draw a diagram like this on the board:

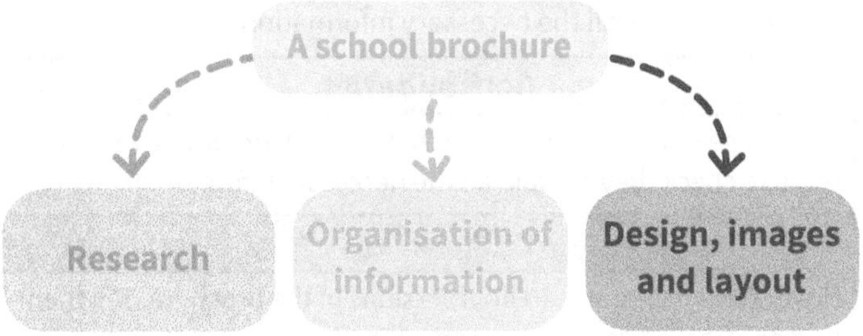

- Discuss the different tasks needed to create a brochure.

  Research: *What kinds of rules and responsibilities do different schools have? How will you decide which to include? Who will be responsible for the final decision?*

  Organisation of information: *What is the purpose of the brochure? What sections will it have? What are the main and supporting details for each section? How will you present the information (bulleted lists, subtitles, numbers, etc.)? Who will be responsible for organising the information?*

  Design, images and layout: *What can make the brochure attractive or easy to read? Where can you find images? Do the images match the information in the texts? Who will select the images and decide on the layout?*

- Encourage students to take notes and share roles and responsibilities.

Step 2: Research and analyse p103 p71

- Have groups start the PLAN section in **Exercise 4**. Tell them to choose one or two of the ideas for why their school is special. Encourage them to make their decisions together.
- Hand out a copy of the > Brochure organiser p65 to each student. Tell them to write their school name at the top.

Flipped classroom activity

Out of class: have students make notes in their organisers.

In class: have groups check their ideas together and agree on which information to include in their final brochures. Have them vote on the best rules and decide on students' responsibilities. Monitor the activity to check everyone has got a part of the brochure to work on.

Step 3: Draft and review p103 p71

Flipped classroom activity

Out of class: have students write their section of the brochure at home.

In class: have groups check their ideas together. Ensure they are giving feedback and making final decisions together. Have groups draft the first version of their brochure. Remind students to include examples of unit language (***can***, ***can't***, ***must***, ***mustn't***, ***have to*** and ***don't have to***), especially in the sections related to roles and responsibilities.

Critical Thinking

Synthesising ideas and information

As groups complete Step 3, make sure they are dividing their work into clear sections and not repeating or leaving out information. Have them check each other's ideas.

> Peer-evaluation form p69 **Development**

3 Production

Schedule presentation times and stick to them, so all groups have time to introduce their brochures and to walk around, read each other's work and ask questions.

As groups work on their final drafts, share ideas about how best to present the brochures. For example, they could present it as a poster or a bi-fold or tri-fold leaflet (see Level 1). > Presentation ideas p19

As students complete their projects, check their abilities in the following Areas of Competency.

Collaboration

Listening respectfully and responding constructively to others' contributions

Listens to and acknowledges different points of view respectfully.

Evidence: Students participate in the decision-making process and respond to different ideas.

Is ready to justify, adapt and abandon a proposal or point of view in response to others' queries or contributions.

Evidence: Students make changes to working drafts based on discussions held during the decision-making process.

Critical Thinking

Synthesising ideas and information

Selects key points from diverse sources to create a new account and/or argument.

Evidence: Group members look at each other's notes and choose the most appropriate ideas to create a brochure.

Step 1: Prepare pp102–103 p71

- Go through the PRESENT section in **Exercise 7**.
- As groups prepare their final brochure, ask questions. For example: *Have you completed all of the sections? Do you have a list of rules and responsibilities? Can you add any more information? Have you used modal verbs appropriately?*
- Remind groups of the presentation date and how much time each group will have. (See Differentiated instruction activities box for further practice.)

Own it! learning tip

Resolving conflicts

Encourage students to reach a compromise when making final decisions about the content and layout of their brochures. If group members can't agree, ask: *Can you think of an alternative solution?* Have students respond respectfully to each other's ideas.

Differentiated instruction

Support
Help students complete their sections. Review the language and check it contains all the necessary information.
Consolidation
Encourage students to check each other's sections. Encourage them to check they contain all the necessary information.
Extension
Have students proof read final versions of the brochure. Tell them to make final decisions after consulting their group.

Step 2: Present p103

- Draw attention to the CHECK section in **Exercise 6**. Tell the class to think about these questions as they read each other's brochures. Tell them to make notes about why they would like to go to a certain school.
- Have groups present their brochures. Ask one person from each group to tell the class the title of their brochure and who worked on it. Then allow groups to walk around and read each other's brochures. Tell them to write down any questions they may have.

Step 3: Reflect p103

- After the presentations, hold a class discussion on the CHECK questions in **Exercise 6**. Have groups ask any questions they may have about the brochures.
- Why do students want to attend different schools? Have a class vote on the most popular.
- Encourage students to think about each stage of the project process, including positive experiences and things they could improve.

> Peer-evaluation form p69 **Production and Reflection**

Go to the digital collaboration space to set, track and assess students' work, or allow students to share and comment on their own work.

Project evaluation rubric: a school brochure

Use these project-specific descriptors and your own choice of descriptors from the > Evaluation rubric p21 to check students individually or in groups. Make your own evaluation form. > Teacher's evaluation form p70

	4	3	2	1
Creativity	Product contains many creative ideas for features of a school. It lists interesting rules and responsibilities that relate to the features of the school. It has an attractive layout with clear sections.	Product contains some creative ideas for features of a school. It lists rules and responsibilities that are mostly related to the features of the school. It has a fairly attractive layout with some clear sections.	Product contains one or two creative ideas for features of a school. It lists some rules and responsibilities, but not many of them are related to the features of the school. It has a fairly attractive layout, but it is not original and some sections are unclear.	Product does not contain any creative ideas for features of a school. It lists some rules and responsibilities, but none of them are related to the features of the school. It has an unattractive layout and the sections are unclear.
Language use	Product shows excellent use of grammar, punctuation and spelling. It shows excellent use of language from the unit (modal verbs for obligation, permission and prohibition). Project communicates its main ideas clearly with only a few or no mistakes.	Product shows good use of grammar, punctuation and spelling. It shows good use of language from the unit (modal verbs for obligation, permission and prohibition). Project communicates its main ideas clearly but with some mistakes.	Product shows adequate use of grammar, punctuation and spelling. It shows adequate use of language from the unit (modal verbs for obligation, permission and prohibition). Project communicates some of its ideas clearly, but some sections need further explanation.	Product shows poor use of grammar, punctuation and spelling. It doesn't use language from the unit (modal verbs for obligation, permission and prohibition). Project is confusing and almost impossible to understand.

Cambridge Life Competencies Framework

You can also check students' progress in the following foundation layers.

FOUNDATION LAYERS	ABILITIES	ACTIONS
Emotional Development and Wellbeing	• Empathise and build relationships	making decisions together, sharing roles, persuading and informing, resolving conflicts, making suggestions, finding solutions
Discipline Knowledge	• Convince the audience	thinking of unique and interesting ideas, persuading the reader, explaining the solution giving reasons for decisions

Flipped classroom activities

Evaluate

In project groups, have students discuss their completed Peer-evaluation forms and ways to work better as a group. > Peer-evaluation form p69

Out of class: Have students think about their progress at home. > KWL chart p67 **Learned**

In class: Hold a class discussion on what students have learned, using the information from their KWL charts. Ask: *How did making decisions together help you improve your project?* Discuss ideas.

> KWL chart p67 **Learned**

9 THE CULTURE PROJECT

A POSTER

- **Learning outcome:** make a poster about a volunteer programme
- **Skills:** choose a volunteer programme, organise information, decide on design, research facts, check each other's work
- **Resources:** two or more posters about volunteer programmes, Poster organiser p66, My time-management plan p71
- **Evaluation tools:** Project evaluation rubric p57, My learning diary p68, Peer-evaluation form p69, Teacher's evaluation form p70

Unit 9

Before you start

Collect two or three posters about volunteer programmes to show students in class.

1 Preparation

Step 1: Introduce the topic

- Introduce the topic of volunteer programmes after doing the reading exercises. p108 Ask: *What types of programmes do people volunteer for? Where are they? How long do they last? Where can you find information about them? Are volunteer programmes popular holidays? Why/Why not?* Share ideas.
- Show students the posters. Ask: *What interesting information do the posters have? How is the information presented?* Discuss what areas of volunteer work the posters focus on.
- Remind students that posters use text and pictures to get people's attention. Ask: *How is the information divided into sections? What pictures can you see? Would you be interested in volunteering on these programmes? Why/Why not?*
- Ask students to bring a poster (in English) to the next lesson. Have them discuss which posters are most attractive and why.

Step 2: Analyse the model for the project Unit 9

- Have students look at the model. Read the title and look at the pictures. Ask: *Where is the programme? What jobs do you think people will do?* Then have students read the poster to check.
- Check comprehension. Ask: *What is ecotourism? How can volunteers help the environment? What other activities are there? Where will volunteers stay?*
- Ask students to compare the design of the model poster and the examples they brought to class. Ask: *Which ideas would you use for your own poster? Why?* (See Differentiated instruction activities below for further practice.)

Differentiated instruction

Support
Have students write a list of the three most interesting things to do on the poster. Have them work in pairs to agree on their lists.
Consolidation
Have students make a plan for a day on the programme. Have them add details about any of the activities that they choose to do.
Extension
Have students write a letter to the organisers of the programme saying that they are interested in volunteering and why. Tell them to say why they would be good volunteers.

Social Responsibilities

Understanding and discussing global issues

As students analyse the model, discuss why this type of work is important and what other parts of the world have similar issues.

Step 3: *How to* design a poster Unit 9

- Go through the ideas with the class. Have different students say why each idea is important.
- Have students find any things in the model or their own examples that follow the ideas in the *How to* section.
- Check students understand that when they design their posters, they should use the ideas in this *How to* section.

Step 4: Clarify the project Unit 9

- Follow the steps in > The learning stages of project work p10.
- Have groups discuss what people volunteer to do around the world. Encourage them to research different types of volunteer work and then brainstorm a list in the following class.

> My learning diary p68 **Preparation**

> Peer-evaluation form p69 **Preparation**

2 Development

Start this stage as soon as groups know their learning outcomes and have brainstormed different types of volunteer programme.

Step 1: Assign roles and responsibilities

- In project groups, have students share general roles > Roles and responsibilities p16. Help them decide on further roles they can share, such as:

The **writer** produces the text and suggests titles.

The **proof reader** checks spelling, grammar and punctuation.

The **graphic designer** arranges the images on the poster.

The **illustrator** adds borders, fonts and suggests colours.

The **picture manager** chooses the images.

Step 2: Research and analyse Unit 9 p71

- Have groups do the PLAN section from **Exercise 1**. Have them select a volunteer programme they are interested in and decide on a name for it.
- Hand out a copy of the > Poster organiser p66 to each student.

Learning to Learn

Practical skills for participating in learning

As students complete Steps 2 and 3, monitor how well individuals are working within their groups and if they are also working well at home.

Flipped classroom activity

Out of class: have students make notes in their organiser. Tell them to find as much information as they can for each section and discuss where they can find information.

In class: have students compare the information in their organisers and agree on which is the most interesting. Allow time for them to discuss the design of their poster and then tell them to share a section for each group member to prepare.

Step 3: Draft and review Unit 9 p71

Flipped classroom activity

Out of class: have pairs write the first draft of their part of the poster at home. Remind them to find interesting pictures.

In class: have groups check each other's work. Encourage them to focus on grammar, punctuation and spelling.

Out of class: if necessary, have students rewrite their parts of the poster at home. Then repeat the above process in class with their second drafts.

Own it! learning tip

Peer-tutoring

Monitor groups as they correct and edit each other's work. Explain that this includes checking spelling, punctuation and language as well as checking that the information is presented in a logical order in the correct sections with interesting images. Encourage students to suggest changes to each other's work and help each other make changes where necessary. Help them with useful language such as: *Why don't you ... ?, You could ..., Maybe you should change this.* Make sure students are giving feedback.

> My learning diary p68 **Development**

> Peer-evaluation form p69 **Development**

3 Production

Schedule presentation times and stick to them, so that each group can present their posters. Spread the presentations over a few lessons, if necessary. Allow enough time for each presentation and for questions.

Before groups produce their final drafts, ask them how they will present the information on their posters. They may want to design their posters in the form of an advert.

> Presentation ideas p19

As students prepare and present their projects, check their abilities in the following Areas of Competency.

Social Responsibilities

Understanding and discussing global issues

Is aware of different global issues.

Evidence: Groups brainstorm possible volunteer programmes covering a variety of issues.

Understands the importance of international cooperation.

Evidence: Groups identify and understand reasons why different programmes are necessary.

Learning to Learn

Practical skills for participating in learning

Completes homework as required.

Evidence: Students complete out-of-class activities and fulfil their roles within the group.

Participates sensibly and positively in learning activities in class.

Evidence: Groups check each other's work and make sensible suggestions for improvements.

Step 1: Prepare Unit 9 p71

- Go through the PRESENT section in **Exercise 2.**
- As groups prepare their final project, ask questions: *Has your poster got photos, maps and drawings? Does it give details about the type of work volunteers can do? Does it provide details about accommodation? Are the sections clearly divided? Is the handwriting clear?*
- Have groups work together to prepare their poster.
- Encourage students to practise and time their presentation. Tell students to each present the section they worked on.
- Remind groups of the presentation date and how much time each group will have.

Step 2: Present Unit 9

- Draw attention to the CHECK section in **Exercise 3.** Ask the class to think about which programme is most interesting and why as they listen to each other's presentations.
- Have groups present their posters. Remind speakers to look at their audience and ask for questions at the end of their presentation.
- Have the class ask questions at the end of each presentation. Encourage group members to help each other.
- Have groups display their posters on the walls after presenting and allow the class time to walk around and look at each poster more closely.

Step 3: Reflect Unit 9

- After the presentations, hold a class discussion on the CHECK questions in **Exercise 3.**
- Have the class discuss what they liked best about the posters. Ask: *Which volunteer programme would you like to take part in? Why?* Then, hold a class vote on the most interesting programme.
- Encourage students to think about each stage of the project process, including positive experiences and things they could improve.

> Peer-evaluation form p69 **Production and Reflection**

Go to the digital collaboration space to set, track and assess students' work, or allow students to share and comment on their own work.

Project evaluation rubric: a poster

Use these project-specific descriptors and your own choice of descriptors from the > Evaluation rubric p21 to check students individually or in groups. Make your own evaluation form. > Teacher's evaluation form p70

	4	3	2	1
Creativity	Product is very well organised with creative and interesting ideas. It has a short and interesting title and all the key information. It has a very attractive design, clear handwriting and eye-catching photos, maps and drawings.	Product is organised with interesting ideas. It has a short and interesting title and most of the key information. It has an attractive design, fairly clear handwriting and eye-catching photos, maps and drawings.	Product has interesting ideas but lacks organisation. It has a title and some key information. It includes photos, maps and drawings, but the design is not attractive and the handwriting is not always clear.	Product lacks interesting ideas and organisation. It is missing a title and/or key information. It is not clear, has an unattractive design and the visuals are not related to the topic.
Language use	Shows excellent use of grammar, spelling and punctuation. Project communicates its main ideas clearly with only a few mistakes.	Shows good use of grammar, spelling and punctuation. Project communicates its main ideas clearly but with some mistakes.	Shows adequate use of grammar, spelling and punctuation. Project communicates some of its ideas clearly, but some sections need further explanation.	Shows poor use of grammar, spelling and punctuation. Project is confusing, poorly written and not clear.

Cambridge Life Competencies Framework

You can also check students' progress in the following foundation layers.

FOUNDATION LAYERS	ABILITIES	ACTIONS
Discipline Knowledge	• Convince the audience	demonstrating knowledge (of destination, activities, etc.), giving specific details, providing interesting information and supporting details, answering questions
Emotional Development and Wellbeing	• Empathise and build relationships	peer-tutoring and giving constructive feedback, helping others complete their tasks, agreeing on content, making suggestions

Flipped classroom activities

Evaluate

In project groups, have students discuss their completed Peer-evaluation forms and ways to work better as a group. > Peer-evaluation form p69

Out of class: Have students think about their progress at home. > My learning diary p68 **Production**

In class: Hold a class discussion on what students have learned, using the information from their learning diaries. Ask: *What do you like about your posters? What things can you improve? What new skills and information have you learned? How can your group work better in the next project?*

> My learning diary p68 **Production**

PRESENTATION ORGANISER

Part 1

Problem	Solution

Part 2

Problem: ______________________________

Background/Effects of problem	
Solution	
Result	
Useful phrases (introductions, describing past events, etc.)	
Ideas for images	

PROFILE ORGANISER

Part 1: General information

Name: ______________________ **Art form:** ______________________

Nationality: ______________________

Education: ______________________

Interests: ______________________

Type of art: ______________________

____

Exhibitions: ______________________

____

Ideas for images	Sources

Part 2: Further details

Interesting facts	Text
Questions	

LANGUAGE FACT FILE ORGANISER

Country	
Population	
Main language	
Other languages	
Total number of languages	
Common expressions	
Interesting fact	
Famous singer or writer	
Favourite word	
Alphabet – any new letters that aren't in your alphabet	

Ideas for images (flags, maps, people, etc.)

REPORT ORGANISER

Purpose	Questions

Classmates' answers/problems they talk about	Your ideas/solutions
	1 2 3 4 5

Presentation ideas

MAGAZINE ARTICLE ORGANISER

Spidergram

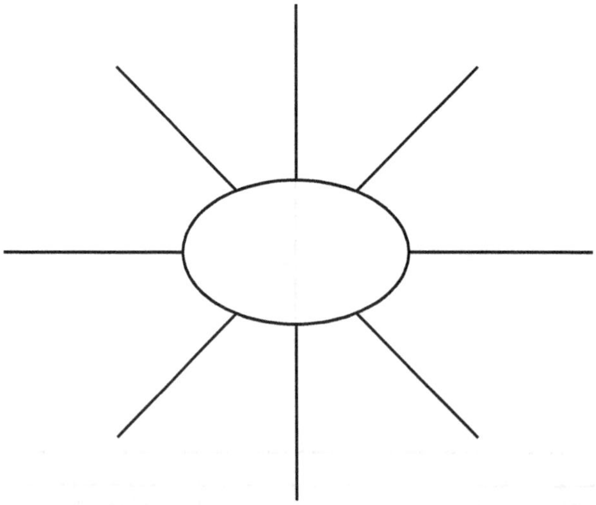

Notes organiser

Title:		
General introduction:		
Introduction	**Main body**	**Conclusion**

INVENTION ORGANISER

1 List of problems

2 Solutions

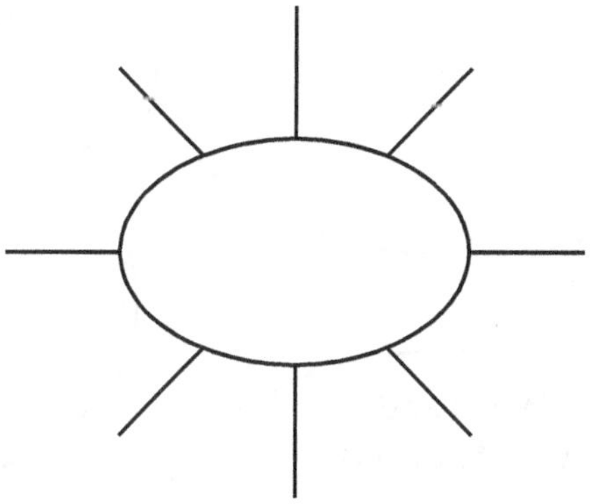

3 Picture of invention

Materials:

4 Picture of how it works

Explanation:

TRAVEL BLOG ORGANISER

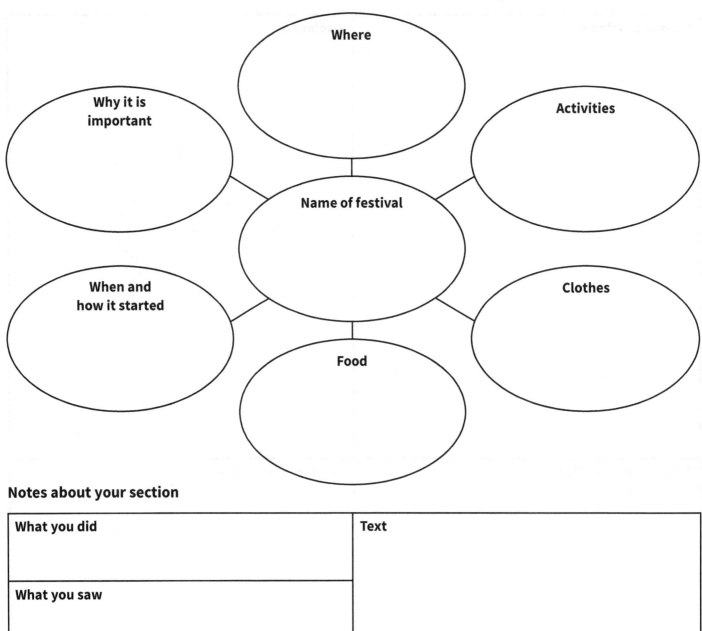

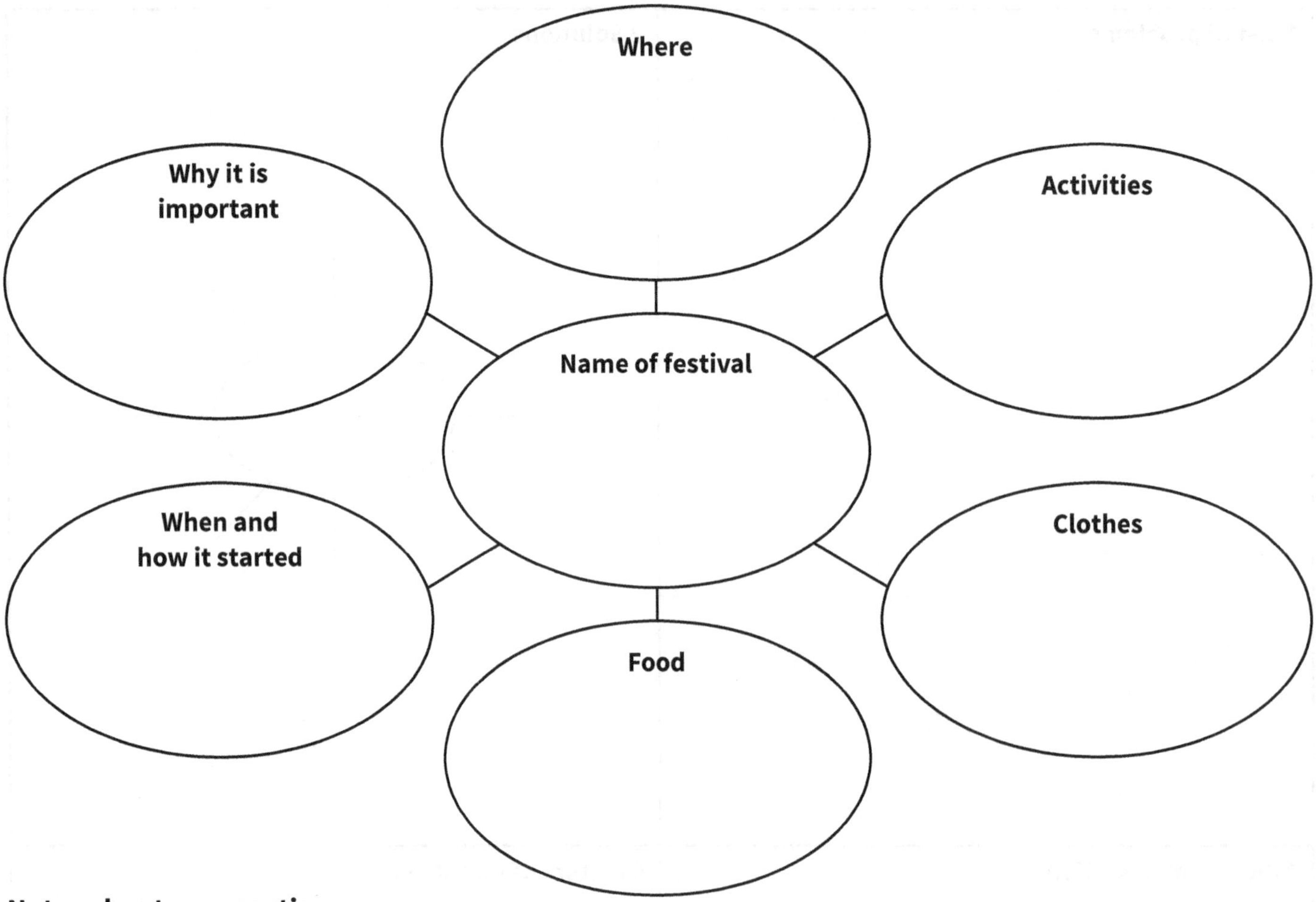

Notes about your section

What you did	Text
What you saw	
Feelings	
Other details (surprising, interesting, etc.)	

Ideas for images:

BROCHURE ORGANISER

Name of school:

Introduction
(why people should come to your school)

Unique features
(what makes your school special)

Student rules

Student responsibilities
(things students should do to help the school be a success)

POSTER ORGANISER

Volunteer programme:

Location:

Reason why the programme is important:

Activities you can do on the programme:

Cultural and other activities:

Accommodation:

Ideas for images:

Name: ______________________________

Date: ______________________________

Unit, topic and project: ______________________________

KWL CHART

Know	Want to know	Learned (Know now)
What do we know about the topic?	*What do we want to know about the topic?*	*What do we know now about the topic?*
		What do we know now about the tasks?
What are our tasks?		*What can we do now as a group?*

Name: ______________________________

Date: ______________________________

Unit, topic and project: ______________________________

MY LEARNING DIARY

1 PREPARATION

- *What am I learning?*
- *What can I use? (for example, the internet, the library, magazines, …)*
- *Who is in my project group?*
- *What is my role in the group?*

2 DEVELOPMENT

- *What is difficult about this project?*
- *Who or what can help me?*
- *What do I like/don't I like?*
- *How can we make our work better?*

3 PRODUCTION

- *Is it a good presentation? Why/Why not?*
- *In the presentation, what is my role?*
- *How do I feel when I give a presentation?*

Name: ______________________________

Date: ______________________________

Unit, topic and project: ______________________________

PEER-EVALUATION FORM

1 **In your group, evaluate your performance. Mark (✓) the columns.**

1 PREPARATION	🙂	😐	☹️
We listen to the instructions.			
We understand the project.			

2 DEVELOPMENT	🙂	😐	☹️
We participate 100% in the project.			
We work well as a group.			

3 PRODUCTION	🙂	😐	☹️
We answer questions about our work.			
We ask questions about others' work.			

REFLECT

2 **Write one good thing about this project.**

____

____

____

____

3 **How can your group work better in the next project? Write one idea.**

____

____

____

____

Name: ______________________________

Date: ______________________________

Unit, topic and project: ______________________________

TEACHER'S EVALUATION FORM

Group or individual performance grades for the selected ✓ general areas.
Grades are as follows: 4 = Exceeds expectations, 3 = Very good, 2 = Good, 1 = Needs improvement.

✓	Areas/Outcomes	Grade	✓	Areas/Outcomes	Grade
	Learning outcomes			Creativity	
	Planning and organisation			Problem-solving skills	
	Use of information and resources			Language use	
	Collaboration (Teamwork)			Presentation skills	
	Time management			Final product	

Group or individual performance grades for the project-specific areas.
Grades are as follows: 4 = Exceeds expectations, 3 = Very good, 2 = Good, 1 = Needs improvement.

Project-specific area	Grade
1	
2	
3	
4	
5	

Cambridge Life Competencies Framework

[Student's name/Group] ______________________________ showed (✓) did not show (✗) development in the following competencies and skills during this project.

Competency 1	✓/✗	Foundation layers	✓/✗
		Emotional development and Wellbeing	
		Digital Literacy	
Competency 2	✓/✗	Discipline Knowledge	
		Comments:	
Comments:			

Overall grade: __________

General comments:

Area(s) of improvement:

Name: ____________________

Date: ____________________

Unit, topic and project: ____________________

MY TIME-MANAGEMENT PLAN

What tasks do you need to do for each step? Write them below, and write the time prediction. Then tick (✓) each task as you complete it and write the actual time it takes.

Research and analyse

What do I need to do?	Time prediction	Actual time
1 ☐ ____________________	→ ________	→ ________
2 ☐ ____________________	→ ________	→ ________
3 ☐ ____________________	→ ________	→ ________

Draft and review

What do I need to do?	Time prediction	Actual time
1 ☐ ____________________	→ ________	→ ________
2 ☐ ____________________	→ ________	→ ________
3 ☐ ____________________	→ ________	→ ________

Prepare

What do I need to do?	Time prediction	Actual time
1 ☐ ____________________	→ ________	→ ________
2 ☐ ____________________	→ ________	→ ________
3 ☐ ____________________	→ ________	→ ________

Reflect

Answer the questions.

- I manage my time well during my project work. ☐ Yes. ☐ Can be better.
- I have time to complete self-evaluation tools for each stage. ☐ Yes. ☐ No.
- How can I improve my time management in the next project?

____

____

____

Acknowledgements

The authors and publishers acknowledge the following sources of copyright material and are grateful for the permissions granted. While every effort has been made, it has not always been possible to identify the sources of all the material used, or to trace all copyright holders. If any omissions are brought to our notice, we will be happy to include the appropriate acknowledgements on reprinting and in the next update to the digital edition, as applicable.

Key: Int = Introduction.

Photography

The following photographs are sourced from Getty Images.
Int: Hero Images; bonniej/E+; snapshots from *Own It Project Book* pages 30–31, 60 and 71; MachineHeadz/iStock/Getty Images Plus; code6d/E+; ilyast/DigitalVision Vectors; snapshot from *Own It Student's Book 3* page 78; vgajic/E+; RobinOlimb/DigitalVision Vectors; RaStudio/iStock; Wavebreakmedia/iStock; snapshot from *Own It Student's Book 2 pages 102–103*; snapshot from *Own It TRB Culture Project 9*, second page.

Typesetting: TXT Servicios editoriales

Cover design and illustration: Collaborate Agency.

Editing: Andrew Reid